Grieving As Well As Possible

Grieving As Well As Possible

An Insightful Guide to Encourage Grief's Flow,
Navigate Difficult Moments, and Put Your Life
or a Friend's Life Back Together

Mardi Horowitz, M.D.

GreyHawk Publishing
Sausalito, California

Published by GreyHawk Publishing, Studio 342, Industrial Center Building,
480 Gate Five Road, Sausalito, California 94965

Printed in the United States of America.

Publication Design by Sherri Ortegren
Cover art by Mardi Horowitz

While the author has made every effort to provide accurate telephone numbers and
Internet addresses at the time of publication, neither the publisher nor the author
assumes any responsibility for errors, or for changes that occur after publication.
Further, the publisher does not have any control over and does not assume any
responsibility for author or third-party websites or their content.

Contents

Introduction

When you are sorrowful look again in your heart, and you shall see that in truth you are weeping for that which has been your delight. ~Kahlil Gibran

In life, we sustain bereavements and must mourn. Doing so is often automatic. We subconsciously process the bad news and change our inner world to be consistent with our new situation in the outer world. Understanding what is happening in a conscious way can help that unconscious process along, and leads to rebuilding our life along the best available lines.

I aim to help with that understanding and hope I succeed to some degree in aiding reconstruction of a life for you that has positive qualities. The grief process is difficult and often painful, but an important benefit that comes about is that the inevitable changes we experience can strengthen us.

Grieving is going to happen without you deliberately saying to yourself, OK, start it now. You can help it along with conscious reflection and that will be our focus. Grieving usually involves a new assessment and possibly a revision of personal emotional values and what life itself means. Through time, contemplation, and good conversation, you can eventually accept the finality of your loss, rebuild your identity and re-construct your future plans and goals. In time, current concerns and relationships with living people blend with memories involving what was lost.

1

I will focus on the death of a life partner as my primary example. The process and suggestions we will cover can also apply to a wide variety of other serious losses or major relationship ruptures such as divorce and other familial losses. Reactions to a loss may be emotional (anger, guilt, anxiety, sadness, and despair), physical (sleeping problems, changes in appetite, physical problems, or illness), and social (feelings about taking care of others in the family, seeing family or friends, or returning to work).

People, especially those sustaining their first major loss event, may not know what to expect. The event may seem catastrophic, and we do not know the degree to which we may have to reconstruct meanings within our minds and immediate social connectivity.

We can learn more, all of us, about our own responses, coping strategies, and reflections, and that can help us adjust our way of thinking and living after sustaining a loss. The most we can ask of ourselves is to grieve "as well as possible", and that is plenty good enough. While grief's process is automatic, the task of encouraging its flow often requires practice in the sense that we can consciously work with our minds versus only letting the mind work unconsciously.

You may wonder how to use your thinking as you travel along grief's path. It will take time and practice if the idea of reflecting upon what and how you are thinking and feeling is new to you — less so if you are familiar with using your reasoning ability to help yourself. Either way, grieving "as well as possible" involves allowing ourselves to learn, make discoveries, fall short, and to accomplish a bit more with every new attempt. Eventually we reconstruct a view of past, present, and future that takes our loss into account.

The idea that grief is automatic, but that you can take a more or less active role in seeing that it gets done, may not make sense at first. This concept will come up several times in this book. The main point for now is that it's okay at times to work hard to actively push ahead, while at other times, to sit passively and let auto pilot take over for awhile.

In other words, there are varied states and phases, or stages, in going through a process that can be fairly complex because it involves such major changes in what our lives are like. This book is organized by a sequence of going through alterations of what is meaningful to you. We will discuss this in terms of relationships that help maintain your identity and even your self-esteem.

The sequence of discussions in this book covers roughly the sequence of stages in a usual grieving process. The risk in discussing distinct stages of grief is that it can provide others a way to pigeonhole us into a convenient category, and predict how we should progress next. And grief just doesn't work that neatly. We go back and forth; we have our unique situations and individuality. Our goal may be to arrive at some sort of completion but it also is true that we never fully "get over" or forget our lost loved one. The grief process allows us to integrate the memory of our loved one into a more manageable place in our psyche and heart so that we can resume a more functional and bearable existence.

The process of grieving works unconsciously, but to grieve as well as possible, we can help how that happens with conscious reflections. Grief work starts when we try to describe and re-describe what has been lost. This can be a description in one's own mind, as in a diary-like note, and in conversations with others. Such forms of expression can help qualify the loss as something that has really happened.

I am going to repeat important concepts throughout this book. The concept of finality is one of those. You consciously know of a death that has occurred, but your unconscious is the last to fully know this. In fact, some aspects of loss, for a time, can feel very unreal.

For example, for a period of time, starting shortly after the loss of her husband, Susan felt compelled to share the details leading up to his death with family members and close friends. She told them about her last two visits at his bedside, and recited their conversation, word for word. She told about her last exchange with him a few hours before he passed, described soothing him, holding his hand, and reassuring him that it was okay to let go.

This allowed Susan to step back a bit and hear herself speak of the reality of loss again and again, and in doing so, the early sense of unreality hovering around her memory dissipated, like a fog that evaporated with sunlight. The unreal was made real, allowing the start of grief's process.

On the way to what is real, it is helpful to gradually understand and reduce any unrealistic fantasies you may have about the meanings of a loss, or any excessive minimizations or magnification of your feelings and emotions. You may find yourself over-idealizing how things were before your loss, which helps to reduce any anger at the deceased, or any sense of grievance about how things were before a death. You may even find yourself over-estimating or under-estimating the benefits of the loss. These deflections from absolute reality are normal, they occur in everyone, and are not necessarily negative.

By finding reality, I mean finding what is adaptive, and we will be covering this theme repeatedly. It is also common, in some ideal fantasies, for you to expect a loss to become magically restored. Sometimes you may find yourself acting as if the loss will be restored, but you will gradually realize that it is only magical thinking to believe you can somehow go back in time to change the past. If only we could wave a magic wand and transform ourselves to a time in life before the loss! It's more helpful to leave that fantasy to the movies!

The opposite of creating an idealistic mental picture is the tendency to form threatening expectations or stories about why the loss happened. In catastrophic fantasies, you may see a loss as a consequence of some evil deed you did in the past, or you expect only doom ahead for you, in a bleak future without recovery. Your job is to confront and relinquish the irrational illusions in small steps, as you find reality and a new and realistic future plan. Give yourself time, patience, courage, and stamina.

One irrational thought that comes to most of us after the death of a loved one is that the loss can be reversed, that there will be a return, soon, and in this life. When such a thought flashes into the mind, it can be answered by saying to ourselves: "that would be wonderful if it could happen, however, it cannot happen." By repeatedly examining what is real, we come to accept reality rather than being continuously surprised at the absence of a person who has departed.

Simple truths can be profound, but only gradually accepted. To some extent, your world has crumbled and you may not know immediately how to make it coherent and cohesive. This can make you feel very nervous or a little crazy in some states of mind, but know that a return to reality can occur, is indeed already occurring, and that you can endure because the future spring can be quite different from the winter storms of grief.

We grieve for what was and for ourselves as we were. Whether or not we desire to make the journey, we must go through a life-changing passage. The world has changed; otherwise a loss is not a major loss. A new inner version of the new reality has to be developed. This inner narrative is about what was lost, about ourselves in view of the loss, and about the new world for us that can now come into being. For example, the death of a loved one

has a great finality, but it does not mean it is our finality. We have not completed our lives.

Because knowing what to expect can reduce a sense of helplessness, this book is about what such a passage may include, and will include ways to have a new vision for your future, which is a way of rebuilding yourself.

Chapter One
Initial Expectations

As an automatic process, grief proceeds through unconscious mental processes when there are not too many inhibitions blocking the way. It does not have to be forced into starting, or forced into ending. At times sorrows emerge unexpectedly, and one may cry at an inopportune moments. At other times, one may want to cry, but tears will not come to one's eyes. Grief takes time, and may have ups and downs in levels of distress.

❖ *Grieving is a "dose-by-dose" form of adaptation, not an "all or none" or "all done in one sitting" experience.*

Loneliness, with pining for the deceased, is one of the distressing states that may occur during grief. If you can find one, a caring friend provides an important human connectedness, and keeps us from feeling isolated. Sometimes, just sitting in the same room together, or even being under the same roof, provides a much needed emotional salve. Conversation is not always necessary; the music of safe connection is enough.

I suggest that you give yourself the gift of time to work through the grieving process as well as you can, and in doing that, you can restore an even more meaningful appreciation of life. As we move through the throes of sorrow, we can remind ourselves that we will survive it. This is hard to do, because during the earliest stages after a loss we are faced with many demands to cope with the consequences of the loss. More on this later.

Sudden Bad News

If the news of loss comes after a long terminal illness, you may have anticipated the death and even done some thinking about your life afterward. If so, you may have been somewhat more prepared for the shock than if the loss happened unexpectedly. Either way, anticipated or unexpected, the news strikes you.

Learning of a death leaves its own special mark. Your mind may have fired out all kinds of ideas during your early conscious response. Those ideas are stored in your unconscious memory. They may come up again later but be submerged for a time. As mentioned, you are subconsciously containing and starting to process reactions that will take some time to accomplish.

When someone you care about is stricken with a terminal illness, you become painfully aware of the fragility of life, and may think about how uncertain life is. It can change the structure of your existence, strip away your control, and can even impact your desire and ability to hope and plan for the future.

This can also happen when a loved one is in danger. If the beloved is a warrior going into combat, or is in another life-threatening situation, then the heightened chance of loss can also set into motion thoughts and feelings of what will happen if a loss occurs, or, you may hold your breath. After the news of actual loss, irrational thoughts about why it may have happened may emerge, mixed with your rational thoughts. Sorting these out as rational or as irrational may take some time.

Concerns for Yourself and the One Lost

After a death you will wonder about the safety even after death of your loved one. You will wonder about your own safety and may feel fragile, uncertain, and tentative about your new life. You may review your relationship with the deceased during the terminal phase of an illness. You may even attempt to judge yourself. If so, pay attention to any emerging and harsh self criticisms.

Some people feel they were too self-centered, or even selfish, when they had thought "what about me in the future," when it was the other person who was struggling, dying, or even suffering. With that, there may have been feelings of personal vulnerability over the immediate loss of everyday security and normalcy. In this case, it helps to realize quite clearly that this is not an either/or proposition. It is not a matter of thinking of yourself going through a loss OR thinking about what happened to the other. It is a both /and proposition. There is plenty to feel and think about in considering the two topics and more besides.

Grief reactions may also include intense guilt, preoccupations with thoughts of your own feelings of worthlessness, severe apathy and inaction, protracted impairment in work and taking care of yourself, and even having auditory or visual, ghost-like hallucinations such as the return of the deceased person. There is a broad range of reactions to consider at times and because no two people grieve in exactly the same way, there is immense individual variation.

Sorrow helps grief; despair does not. Sorrow says "I mourn", despair says "I give up." Accepting sorrow means, "I can go on; I will never give up." Giving up and giving in to perpetual mourning without let-up are states of mind you may experience, but I hope they will be quite momentary. Please know that over time, human beings have evolved to have tremendous courage and the ability to cope with each new loss. Each of us, in our own minds, can learn how to become resourceful and build the energy and strength to recover by doing the work of grieving.

Finding the Right Coping Strategies

You may find that you grapple with all kinds of coping strategies, both appropriate and inefficient. These are all within the normal range of experiences and not under anyone's full conscious control. It is not a matter of will power to prevent your mind from clouding with unwanted emotions, or to force a cleansing bout of weeping at a funeral service. Rather, as with grief in general, it is a matter of courage and stamina to endure what must be tolerated, and to make easier those difficulties that can be made a bit more manageable without too much emotional cost to others.

To the degree that we can realistically think and feel about what lies ahead, the grief period after a loss can be lightened, but not eliminated. Once again, the real moment strikes its own discordant notes and a darkened passage needs to be negotiated. The trip, however, may be a bit shorter if the loss was not traumatic or very premature in life.

For a time after a loss, you may experience feelings of apathy, insomnia, poor or increased appetite, anxiety, irritability and weight loss or gain. These symptoms are often associated with felling deeply sad, having despairing ruminations, and severe worries.

❖ *If you have suicidal impulses or cannot function, it can mean that you are suffering from a complicated grief reaction and/or a clinical depression. You should promptly seek professional help.*

Protecting Yourself from Damaging Attitudes and Reactions

Death ends a life, not the relationship we carry within. The deceased is not forgotten, and most of the time, death is not a deliberate abandonment. Try to see it as a loss but not the fault of the one you have lost or your own. Perhaps, within the recesses of your mind, both you and the deceased are seeking the grace of forgiveness.

There is a reaction that may eventually lead to trouble, and that is "I cannot bear it". This attitude may derail some grieving processes that could otherwise transform a sense of what is unreal to the realization of what actually happened to you. A more effective attitude to adopt and encourage is, "yes I can bear it; it is painful, and yet, I can bear that."

Once you decide to face the loss and decide to tolerate negative feelings and let your thoughts flow, you can spend some calm time reviewing and completing stories about how and why the loss occurred. You will go back to the less clear and more complicated parts of the story much later on.

Look for Authenticity in Connecting with Others

Sometimes a stricken person can find themselves in the midst of conversations that feel uncomfortable because of the fear of emotions getting out of control. In such instances, it helps if you think of a kind of script ahead of time to help yourself get through such situations. You can practice saying, "Thank you for asking about how I am, but I would prefer not going into how I am feeling inside just now. I know you will understand." You can then divert the conversation by asking about the other person or changing to another topic.

The Value of a Support System: Friends, Acquaintances and Family

You don't need to be embarrassed when you feel a need to use or build up your own support system. A direct request to have a talk in private with a friend or small group of companions can lead to a welcome opportunity to share your distress. Remember, this is a journey, and you may need to pace yourself and rely on others again and again over a period of time.

A support system means practical help, advice, and information of the kind we need. It also means resources such as cash, food, and shelter, and above all, someone to listen and acknowledge you. This is hard to establish if a social network is not already in place.

If you are isolated, the first task is to get out of isolation. You can ask acquaintances at work for a cup of coffee and a conversation. This will not fill all your needs, but it is a meaningful step in reassuring you that human contacts are possible. The computer and telephone also help and resources are listed at the end of this book. When you need help, and none is available, seek out a bereavement support group. You can also bring help into the world by offering to help others. This, at least, restores a measure of pride and hope.

In general, family is nature's support system. In reality this may not be true for you. If there are toxic family members, or those who are exploitative and deceitful, it is best to avoid them.

Even with family members you choose to interact with, there may be complexities to consider. If the loss is in the family, others also have to pace themselves in grief work. What is right for one may be too fast or slow for some others in the family. Part of the conversation can be to share views on the topic of how much to discuss now and what to deal with another time.

Expect to Feel Unstable for Awhile

After a loss, we can no longer depend on the expected order of life as before because it may have turned into chaos. Our sense of feeling in control may have vanished. Our physical and mental resources may feel depleted. Normal life seems remote, even unattainable.

In our darkest moments, we experience separation and isolation, even from those trying to comfort us. How could they possibly understand what we feel? Weighed down by the heaviness of sorrow, we may become pessimistic about the possibility of positive change — regaining a sense of comfort, security, or enjoyment of the simple pleasures of living can seem remote.

Accept that, for a period of time, unexpected changes in mental functions may occur. A memory of the deceased might pass in review unexpectedly while at work or driving. A surge of strong feeling might be triggered by a reminder of the loss. It is important to understand this type of change, and remember that you are not spinning totally out of control. You can't always know when or where you might feel grief-related thoughts, impulses, emotions or moods. Experiencing and tolerating temporary departures from usual states of mind is one of the first steps in learning how to grieve in a way that will soon lead to restored balance in life.

Even though you feel like the world is crumbling into a million little pieces, know that restorative processes can and will occur, and that the extremes in your day to day life will eventually subside. This is difficult to remember because many of us fear that in times of instability and distress our minds will not recover. This is because the severe mental and even physical changes after a loss can lead to intrusive thoughts and intense feelings that disrupt your mental and emotional balance.

Here is one of those points I plan to repeat: in some states of mind you may feel as if you have lost your composure. This is common. It is often a sign of progress in the work of grief — you realize that you are deeply shaken and feel a loss of composure as you begin to digest the loss at a core level within.

Other unusual changes in thought may occur due to inhibitions or deficits in the way you normally reason through your day-to- day activities. You may want to recall a happy memory about the deceased, to hear a voice or see a face in your mind, and be unable to do so. You may wish to cry at a funeral and discover that your reaction is instead, numb and dry eyed.

Mary: Altered Thought Processes

Mary's elderly mother died when Mary was fifty years old. For years prior, they had spoken daily and enjoyed dinner together once a week. Mary felt sorrowful, and cried at the funeral. She took a week off from her work and social activities to go through her mother's belongings, carefully reflecting upon memories. Feeling good, she resumed her life as usual, until weeks later, she found herself preoccupied with unwelcome images of hostile exchanges with her mother. When Mary tried to deliberately recall pleasant, loving memories of her mother she could not conjure up any image of her mother's face.

Later on, Mary regained full control over her internal storehouse of memories by gradually reviewing and reassembling her story of a lifelong connection with her mother. Mary reached into her mind and consciously chose memories from her life that involved her mother and practiced replaying the new sequence. Various snapshot memories were stored in Mary's memory, and after a time, she was able to more easily recall the new sequence. Mary was telling herself a story that incorporated new facts and some new interpretations into her life narrative, as she had lived and recalled it so far. With this intertwining of fragments into her story, she had greater control of her conscious thoughts. Now, she could, at will, visualize her mother's face. The restoration of Mary's positive memories happened after she had consciously helped herself progress further along the process of grieving.

Numbing

Grief's process can include numbness and denial, often the first reaction to a loss. Don't be surprised if you feel numb while others are crying. Numbness can help cushion the blow and can help you get through the initial mourning rituals with the family. The numbness wears off, and the painful realization of the loss may hit full-force; you may yearn deeply for your lost loved one and be angry and have regrets of things left unsaid or dreams never realized.

Gradually, reorganization and the beginning of positive emotions start to take place. Over time, you can start to perceive your life in a more positive light, although bouts of grief and sadness may come back from time to time for several years.

Points to Remember

- Compassion is the watchword, for yourself as well as for others.

- Tell others how to be compassionate for your feelings.

- Expect to feel unstable for a while after a loss. A reduction or increase in emotion that seems atypical for you may occur. Make every effort to avoid harsh self judgments.

- Waves of uncertainty can be scary, but try not to view them as a loss of yourself, as you are still an effective and competent person.

Chapter Two

First Reactions: Taking Care of Yourself and Your Family

The process of mourning taxes both body and mind. Take care of yourself. This is important from the moment you feel grief's first pang and throughout your grief work. I encourage you to refer to these suggestions, again and again, over time.

It is important to have an outlet for sharing grief, even if you aren't usually comfortable talking about your feelings. Humans are social creatures and knowing that others know and understand will make you feel less isolated within the shell of your pain. Many support groups exist for the general public as well as specific populations, such as grieving parents and suicide survivors. Whatever the nature of your loss, it is likely that connecting with others will help you recover. Some resources to explore are listed at the end of this book.

Try to Keep a Regular Sleeping and Eating Schedule

Try to get enough sleep, at least eight hours, when you can. Often, an extra hour or two beyond your usual length of sleep is needed.

❖ *A regular routine will be of benefit, including habits that quiet you, and it may help to say "sleep time is safe time" before closing your eyes.*

If you are tired during the day, give yourself a chance to sit or lie down. Resting your body will help your emotional recovery because your mental coping mechanisms recharge as you rest.

Eat well. Avoid overeating or missing meals and try to eat healthy, regular meals. Even if it's the furthest thing from your mind, pay attention to the quality of what you eat. Take the time to eat meals while sitting down, and don't rush through meals, even though you may be pressed for time and do not feel like cooking.

Eating a healthy diet is a natural way to regulate and sustain your energy — all important as you experience and encourage grief's process. Healthy snacks such as fresh fruit or yogurt will help your resolve to eat well by keeping you satiated. Snacks should be nutritious and filling.

You may want to take care of meal preparation ahead of time, or ask a friend to help you with that task. Call a trusted friend and suggest sharing a meal together at least once per week and make a standing date. Sharing meals at regular intervals can provide an opportunity to eat and talk, or simply sit quietly in the company of a friend.

Self Expression

It may be important to allow yourself some off-duty time. Music and crafts can be a comfort.

Start or continue writing in a journal or diary. Be as honest as possible about how you feel. By doing so, you are helping your unconscious mind face what has happened. Honest assessment brings about admission and acceptance of the loss, and, in turn, your psyche will follow in accepting a new reality, a little at a time. You may want to create an artistically-inspired memento about your loved one.

This may be a good opportunity to reflect on the good times — appreciate the contributions of your loved one, and recall moments together that you cherish. Do things to honor and remember your loved one: if they loved flowers, plant a garden in their honor or help others plant gardens; support the causes and organizations that were important to your loved one.

Avoid Medicating Yourself

Avoid self-medicating with drugs, alcohol, or cigarettes. Though you may crave a chemical to help you get through this time, try your best to steer clear of these substances because their side effects can be unhelpful in the long term. For instance, avoid increasing your intake of caffeine or other stimulant substances. The short term jolt is not in your best interest. The sudden rush of energy and the inevitable crash afterward can undermine your ability to cope with your emotions and the tasks at hand through the early days after a loss.

Pay Attention to How You Feel and Look

Pay some attention to your sense of self, including how your body, face and hair look, as well as how your voice is sounding. Make yourself feel and look as upbeat and healthy as is possible. Even though you may feel low, assuming an upbeat attitude for a time can provide you with a respite from your inner pain.

Exercise Regularly

Try to work towards feeling more solid and centered. For example, practicing yoga or light exercise can help to restore a feeling of solidity and balance.

If you are physically able, take a brisk walk in the morning or at lunchtime. Choose something that will motivate you to get out of bed. Whether you feel like it or not, get some sort of physical exercise every day.

Connect with Friends

Here is another repeatable point: most friends want to help you get through this time. Accept help from friends when it feels right.

❖ *It's all right to tell friends how they can best help you.*

Plan Ahead

Anniversaries and holidays bring their own particular challenges. You may feel especially emotional each year on the day that your loved one died, on their birthday or another significant marker.

As a Parent, Helping Children and Teenagers Understand Grief

If you have children, they may have a high priority for your help shortly after news of a loss. You may even postpone some work within yourself in order to make sense of what will happen from your child's perspective. Taking the time to address their concerns early can be a relief for you and reassuring for them. Here is some general advice.

Children and teenagers grieve, but not in the way some adults may expect. Even on breaking the news of a loss to a young person, the initial response may seem unusual to an adult. The child may seem to move quickly to self oriented issues, such as "so who will take care of me now?"A child in the family may have more rapidly changing emotions and the tendency to more emotional ups and downs than others. Grief may manifest itself as changes in appetite, behavioral impulses, and sleep habits. These frequent changes in state of mind may lead to unexpected experiences with children, such as a child at a funeral appearing dry-eyed, or perhaps playing or day dreaming, while streams of tears roll down the faces of adults. Even teenagers may appear to be uncaring, because they experience and express their grief in different ways than adults.

Helping Children with Grief

When you help a child who is grieving, encourage him or her to talk about feelings. Children may not be ready to talk about the loss. Be patient and available. Explain that it is all right to laugh and play. It is important that you help your child understand what has happened in his or her own terms and that it is okay to feel sad, angry, guilty, and even to have no feelings at all as they move through their daily activities and life.

Very young children do not fully understand death. Some think of death as temporary. It is, however, important for a child to realize some of the realities of death, and it is important for adults to use a shared language rather than metaphors that suggest that it is only a transitory condition. Terms such as "went to sleep" and "passed on" suggest that the deceased has departed but may return soon. That may calm a child but it does not help a child to accept the reality of a loss and may lead to eventual disappointments.

A child may have questions that adults think have already been answered. When a child asks if there has been a death, it should be answered by saying that a death has occurred in a language that the child can understand. You can give circumstances of the death without out too many details. For example, you can say, "Dad was in an accident and died." Then you can ask the child if they have any questions and try to answer them simply, directly, truthfully and as calmly as possible.

Children also do not know about the different memorials and ceremonies that help people mourn as individuals, families, and within their communities. You may tell them what customs are, and it can be helpful for them to hear suggestions of personal activities they might do to show their concern and commemoration as a form of paying respect to the lost loved one. For example, you may suggest planting a flower or tree, or painting a picture, writing a poem, or even dedicating a place where they can remember the deceased.

A child may also receive confusing or incorrect information about mourning practices or the nature of death itself, as well as distorted information about the life of the deceased. It is important for a concerned adult to correct this misinformation and provide a realistic picture. This can include sharing a personal perspective about feelings and what might be expected in the future. Sharing in this way can reassure a child that any recurrent or unwelcome images of the deceased are normal.

A child needs a renewed sense of security in trusted adults. A helping adult can provide a child the best chance to get through the process intact by planning a regular schedule and explaining why changes have occurred. Encouraging expression through play, art, music, stories and puppets may be helpful in giving and receiving new information from children and the supportive adults in their lives.

Sometimes children and adolescents who have lost a parent become very anxious that the surviving parent will also die. The child needs to be reassured that they will be well taken care of. Showing affection to the child and fostering an atmosphere of security will allow the child to automatically carry on with their grief process, which often happens unconsciously.

Helping Teenagers with Grief

A teenager is a "tween" as in "in between," and may react to a loss in a manner that is similar to younger children or to adults. While a teenager may be aloof and want to hold back from the family process of sharing a loss, it is just as important as with a child to provide security, regularity, and continuity in an accepting way.

Sometimes, adolescents cope with loss by using avoidance. They secure their own safe places before they carry out some of the harder passages of grief work. They may avoid telling their peers that there has been a death in their family, and may even answer inquiries as if the deceased person is "fine" to get away from the topic. They can be helped by discussing with them that they can still be regarded well by their peers even if they show signs of sorrow, cry, or share the details about what has taken place in their lives.

Here are some suggestions you can consider and put to use when helping children and teenagers with grief:

- Children and teenagers grieve but not at the same pace or trajectory as they will when they become adults.

- Resist being overprotective. It is easy to want to watch the young person's every move and to take over things they normally do themselves. Give them a little space.

- Set limits and rules — and follow through.
  Children and adolescents need structure and boundaries even during difficult times such as the death of a loved one.

- Be available for them when they need you. If they mention the deceased person, there's a good chance they want to talk more about them. Sit and listen.

- Don't be afraid to let your emotions show (to a point). It gives children permission to express their emotions.

- Let children know what to expect, such as how this death will affect them.

- Remember "special days" that affect them (their own birthdays, the lost loved one's birthday, the anniversary of the death, or holidays).

- Be aware of what a young person can and cannot understand. Very small children 0-2 years have no concept of death. They may however notice and respond to their parents' state of heavy grief. Young children often believe that death is not permanent and is reversible. Older children may think that a death is the result of something they or someone else did or failed to do. When children advance to 8 to 12 years of age, they understand the finality of death and that it has a biological basis. Adolescents can be the most challenging to deal with in grief matters. Teenagers sometimes feel their hopes and dreams have been crushed with the death of a loved one.

Understanding how children and teens view death can go a long way in helping them cope with their loss. There are many excellent books that give more details about how to help children and teenagers.

Points to Remember

- Helping your family realize what loss means, and that life goes on, helps you sustain your sense of self as a coherent person and, of course, helps them maintain a sense of "we" with you.

- The beginning is just the beginning. There is more to come and it will occur to you automatically. Getting past the first shock waves is your job in the beginning, and it involves taking good care of yourself.

- You may feel as if you are wounded or damaged. This is probably an exaggeration and you will have more courage and stamina than you expect at this early stage.

Chapter Three
Moving Forward with the Work of Grief

In this chapter I will discuss some generalizations about the early phase of grief work. Our discussion will examine deflections from usual conscious experiences. These deflections include more intrusive thinking and more avoidant or benumbed experiences than usual. However, some people are not bothered with unbidden images or numbing.

Many grieve for a very long time, but in fits and starts. Others move through the passage relatively quickly. If you were able to think about your loss before the actual death occurred, you may be able to move through early grief somewhat more quickly. If not, it will probably take more time. We must not take for granted that those who feel first feel the most. Amongst the group of adults in a family, for example, some experience intrusive waves of feeling while others wait before taking in and understanding the effects of loss. They may not actually cry for weeks or even months. Some freeze in grief — loss dwells like a glacier awaiting safety before feelings thaw.

News of a Loss: Grief's Overture

The news of a loss that has not been fully expected (and what losses are ever fully anticipated?) produces a psychological fracture, a very serious clash between what was previously expected and the actual here-and-now. The conflict, the serious mismatch, brings on strong levels of emotion.

The news of loss may come without notice, for example, by a phone call announcing a terrible accident. The telephone caller may say a life partner has just died. Your mind cannot grasp all the facts. Instead, you may think, "he is now being threatened and harmed! I must rush to help and protect!" This stage may include sudden outbursts that will only be processed later, such as, "It's all my fault!" Or "I can't take it!" Your mind may shout helplessly and soundlessly, "I must prevent it!" Such a contradiction of thoughts, including "he is dead, not dead, must be alive, and I must have him alive" can occur in jumbles. Amongst the hardest states of mind to experience are those of helpless but agitated restlessness in which you desperately want to help the deceased who is, in your mind, being harmed, terrified, dismembered, or suffering torments of isolation rather than being "safely dead" (beyond further harm and beyond terror or despair at being dead) . A person may also go through a time believing that the deceased will return, and have hallucinatory visions of the deceased in ghost-like images.

Funeral rituals counteract these potentially horrifying states, by allowing us to protect the dead and soothe their passage from this world, using symbols such as placing flowers near the grave, or the ritual of using a boat, on which the Norseman would float the burning remains into the twilight of the sea as the sun sets.

Physical reactions during this initial phase are not uncommon. As an example, in James Agee's "A Death in the Family", a young widow is standing before the mirror preparing herself while alone for a social remembrance of her husband who was killed in a car accident. As she turns to go through the door to see other people, she has a searing pang of emotion.

> *"The realization came without shape or definability, save as it was focused in the pure physical acts of leaving the room, but came with such forces, such monstrous piercing weight, in all her heart and soul and mind and body but above all in the womb, where it arrived and dwelt like a cold and prodigious, spreading stone, that groaned almost inaudibly, almost a mere silent breath an ohhhhh, and doubled deeply over, hands to her belly, and her knee joints melted." [Pp.305-a306]*

In the example written by Agee, the physical and mental feelings experienced by the widow were intense and unpleasant. First she was before her mirror, thinking as if in a dream about her loss, and at the difference between her past and future. The topic was painful, and she felt it, but the even more powerful wave of feelings had not yet arrived. That surge of emotion happened as she went through the doorway from the room where she could reflect on her own and stepped outside her home into the community, and to the gathering where others would see her. When she changed rooms, she understood the deep reality of her loss. The death of her husband was not a painful fantasy; it was an inexorable reality. All the unresolved, undigested, and fearsome topics and the enormity of her loss moved from "maybe" to "it is so." The strong feelings of this early phase of reaction to a loss may come as actions and images, as well as words.

Earlier, I mentioned the sudden rush of ideas that may surge into consciousness with the first news or early reminders of what has happened. These may include exclamations such as appeals for divine help ("Oh God!") or expressions of rage ("God damn it!") or remorse ("I'm so sorry!"). Some form of denial can also occur in this phase ("Oh no! It can't be! Say it isn't so!"). A rapid appraisal of yourself during this early phase leads to conscious vows like "I will survive this," or "I will never enjoy life again – ever!" or even "It is all my fault!" These inner declarations become an important part of the memory to be reconsidered and reevaluated.

You are neither consciously aware nor able to predict when spontaneous images, intrusive thoughts, anxious dreams, or pangs of emotion will occur. Just as the crescendo of this experience is not predicted or called up by conscious choice or deliberate intention, the decrescendo is usually not the result of a conscious choice. While you may come to know that a reminder can trigger a pang of emotion, you cannot predict when waves of emotion will take place, or for how long a sorrowful mood might persist. It is helpful to understand that grief work is progressing unconsciously.

This unconscious process, grief work, is associating, that is, linking together, news of change with long standing memories. With a vitally important loss, your mental map of the world is being modified. This continues, usually in a healing way, off and on, while you are awake and in dreams as you sleep.

Understanding Denial and Detachment in the Early Phases

We expect sorrow and yearning after a loss. The death of a loved one has too much substance and meaning to fully process in a short time. We do not expect to feel detached, but that can also be a phase of responding to the loss. Don't be surprised if you feel numb while others are crying. Numbness or shock can help cushion the blow and can help you get through the initial mourning rituals with the family.

Until you feel a sense of security after a loss, you may automatically (that is unconsciously) avoid thinking about the implications of the loss. In a way, the various topics to consider in the future, "dose-by-dose," are lined up unconsciously, for you to knowingly accept at a later time. These unresolved topics will come up again in the near future. I will discuss this again in a later chapter.

First, you deal with immediate survival needs, and then later, with the long term implications. For example, Morris and Boris were identical twins. They were inseparable until after 9/11, when one joined the army and the other enlisted in the air force. Their father had died prematurely of a heart attack just a few weeks before they decided to volunteer. Boris was injured in an explosion during training. After his twin's accident, Morris seemed to have amnesia about his father's death for several weeks. He felt depersonalized and at first, unworried about Boris. Memories of his father popped into his mind only after it became clear that Boris would be all right. Then, he realized how deeply worried he had been that he might also lose Boris to death.

Coping with Emotions

By now, you are familiar with the previously mentioned stages of grief which may include times of denying or arguing with fate, fear, sorrow, and anger. These stages may begin with an initial period of avoiding the significant consequences of the loss, or the importance of the loss to yourself, as well as a sense that you are, emotionally numb. Soon, however, you may experience surges of feeling. Prepare yourself for unanticipated waves by knowing that your thinking and emotional processes are extensive and only partially in your reflective awareness. Changes in your worldview are moving forward. As time passes, you will regain a sense of being in control of your mind.

Recognizing Emotional "Threads"

One way you might want to organize and understand your emotions is to use a metaphor, visualizing red, green, and blue threads. The idea is to follow the thread through the fabric of your experiences over time.

Usually we have medleys of emotion, not just a single feeling, like pure anger. As an example, anger for you can be different than anger for me. For me, anger is usually a feeling of tension, irritability, hostility, sarcasm, and disappearance of my sunny disposition. My irritability conceals a potential mood of sadness. I use the metaphor of threads to cover a medley of typically connected feelings. You will get to know about your own medley by following the threads of emotional components.

Paying attention to emotional threads gives you just a bit more self-control. Naming an emotion helps us learn how and why we are experiencing an emotional state of mind. States come and go and we can learn what triggers the change, what has shifted within or without. Most important, just naming is a bit of knowing, and that self-understanding increases a sense of control, even during distress.

Red (Anger)

Follow the red thread of anger. Loss has many consequences such as struggling with daily tasks by yourself, handling financial decisions that were once shared, and learning to be alone — any or all of these can increase irritability. Any assault on your well being, such as getting a parking ticket, will increase your frustration. You may experience a natural but raw response: hostility.

Angry emotions may not be realistically targeted; they are often unfairly displaced onto people or objects that are convenient and near. It helps to pay attention to, and deal with this red signal. You can control a flare of temper in its early stages. A hostile remark may come to mind, but at the same time, you know that it would not be fair to verbally abuse others.

Fairness and blame are strange but important themes during grief work. Your ideas about what is fair in life may conflict with the new blunt reality that losses are not fairly distributed. One exercise you can try in facing anger with more calm is to look at your explanations when you find yourself blaming others, perhaps even including the deceased. Some of our mental stories can be quite unrealistic. Clearly stating them allows us to re-examine and find the difference between probable and improbable explanations of what seemed to have happened in our memory stories.

For example, Ken kept thinking about the poorly constructed machine gun he had been firing. If the inventor had given it a better firing mechanism, his buddy Sam might have survived the battle. This amounted to an irrational fantasy of who was to blame, and provided a target for blame and self-disgust. For a time, putting blame on the inventors helped Ken feel strong in his indignation. Ken felt righteously upset with someone else who had not been careful enough, but Ken could also have been wondering if he had been careful enough in protecting Sam from risks. Even when there is no personal fault, for Ken, the question "how might I have been to blame?" may have to be considered eventually even though the enemy killed Sam.

Within ourselves, we all carry with us childlike beliefs about why bad things may happen. Now is a time to gradually accept and then correct any childish beliefs. For many losses, no one person or cosmic force is to blame.

Green (Fear)

Face the green thread of fear. Fear can be helpful because it motivates preparation for danger, but it can grow to irrational proportions. We fear that at any moment there may be another hammer blow or sudden loss such as that which we have already experienced.

As with anger, use the fear signal as an indicator of where to pay constructive attention. Try to clearly bring up the ideas involving the threat. For example, after an earthquake, you may feel scared to go into a garage because it had similar girders to the ones on the freeway that had collapsed and crushed cars during the earthquake. You might master the phobia of entering that garage or you might instead, park many blocks away from your work. Clarify your fear — in this example, your safety feels threatened. Then, rationally examine how much danger might lurk in the garage versus walking a long distance in the dark, after work, down that street to your parked car.

Realistic fear can be important in helping us prepare, should such a threatening event occur. Unrealistic fears, however, are common. Correct irrational and unhealthy thought sequences by using your reasoning ability to rehearse reasonable conclusions. The old thought patterns will eventually lessen, and even disappear. With time, if the same pang of fear recurs, your new beliefs will come to mind first.

For example, Martha was unable to sleep because she was afraid that she would be needed in the night to administer pain medication to her recently deceased husband. Night after night, she lay awake, afraid that she wouldn't hear his call for help. Finally, Martha got a hold of her inner voice and said, "Stop. Don't go there. Ben is no longer here and it's okay for me to sleep now. I can sleep until morning and I will feel better."

Martha might only sleep for an hour before waking up again, but this kind of mental re-programming to restore equilibrium happens a bit at a time. In this instance, Martha is actively "grieving as well as possible." In awhile, matters will improve. Martha may still awaken with a feeling of anxiety, but once awake, the anxiety may dissipate more quickly because of the calming self-talk. Further along in time, sound sleep may be fully restored.

Blue (Sadness)

Accept sadness and consider its meaning in small doses when you are relatively calm and it is safe to experience your emotions with the thoughts that seem to evoke them. Sorrow is usually based on a mismatch between hopeful expectations and a loss that is realized. Eventually, the discrepancy between your hoped for return of a deceased person and reality will be reduced, although probably not eliminated. With time, you can unpack your bag of sorrows, and there will be more than one item in the mix. You miss the deceased person, but you also miss activities such as cooking together, attending concerts or events that you shared with the other person. Try to consider one item of loss at a time, and start rebuilding a future. For example, Morgan was dependent on his salary and that of his life partner Grover to pay the monthly mortgage on their house. After Grover died, Morgan faced a foreclosure on his house because he could not afford the large monthly payment on his own. He felt desperate but knew he had to maintain a rational attitude. He found out how to renegotiate his financial situation, a function that Grover had previously managed. Once he completed this, the threat of suddenly losing his home lessened.

Paradoxically, it seemed, when the threat of home loss was reduced, Morgan had more pangs of sadness, crying about Grover not being at home for dinner. Focusing on the obvious can help: Morgan thought "I really miss him when the time comes to cook together!" He was able to face the impact of the loss of closeness, domestic partnership, and source of mutual understanding. While distressed, he felt more in control of how and when he experienced his massive sorrow.

As you consider sources of sadness or sorrow, here are some other ways to handle distress.

- Pay attention to little bits of progress, such as feeling more courage and stamina.

- Examine work and social patterns from time to time. Consider taking up your work more fully and resuming social connections that you may have dropped for a time. Work and relationships bolster your own sense of identity and life as worth living.

- Plan to detect and counteract a sense of apathy about what is going on. Life can seem very gloomy during grief and you must make every effort to defeat that heavy dullness. Getting out of the home to accomplish a short errand can be a courageous act to take some pride in. If this is not the time to tackle tasks requiring extended periods of mental concentration or focus, wash the dishes, putter in the garden, or alphabetize the files. Activity feels better than apathy once you get started.

Modifying Belief Systems, Early Phases

Loss is seldom a single event. It is a rope that unravels into many strands. Each strand consists of many fibers. There are many emotions and habits entwined in a single loss. While some feelings are positive, as in a sense of liberation from care-taking responsibilities, most are negative, as you think about all the activities that you did with the departed one and now, are no longer possible.

Every system of faith considers the issue of death, and questions about its finality are addressed. Your own spiritual beliefs may be awakened. For some, during grief, dormant ideas may now be reconsidered and perhaps reconstructed, especially in those who have not gone through a loss before. To some extent, this will automatically happen as you move through grief's process. For now, if you have organized rituals, such as taking care of others who are close to you by providing food, or asking for help as you plan a memorial, it can provide welcome structure to your life. If you have a faith, seek guidance from others in your spiritual community. The most positive action you can take is to embrace your faith, if you have a belief system in place, or reach out to those you trust for comfort and guidance.

Early Phase Social Expectations and Rituals of Mourning

We expect friends, family and society to offer assistance, consolation and support to the bereaved, but there are some responses that may not provide what is needed. For example, pity is not necessarily a healing balm.

Generally, pity is the sympathy and sorrow we feel by the misfortune, affliction or suffering of another. Pity often implies a feeling of compassion which moves us to help a bereaved friend or family member and relieve them in any way we can.

In 1939, Stephen Zweig wrote these words as the front piece of his book "Beware of Pity" (London: Cassell, translated by Phyllis and Trevor Blewitt, 1939):

"There are Two Kinds of Pity"

One, the weak and sentimental kind, which is really no more than the heart's impatience to be rid as quickly as possible of the painful emotion aroused by the sight of another's unhappiness, that pity which is not compassion, but only an instinctive desire to fortify one's own soul

against the sufferings of another: and the other, the only kind that counts, the unsentimental but creative kind, which knows what it is about and is determined to hold out, in patience and forbearance, to the very limit of its strength and even beyond."

Part of understanding the effect we can have on others as we grieve is that there may be times when our friends may create physical or emotional distance from us because we remind them that the sword of loss hangs by a thread above us all.

Most of us live in a cocoon of our daily lives, oblivious to the transience of life. Being with us as we grieve perforates their denial of death. Walling us off, however, deprives us of some real support.

While extraordinarily helpful, in and of itself, friends who engage with genuine empathy can exhaust themselves. When the need for a break occurs, encourage your friends to take time to restore themselves, while still maintaining a regular and valuable intermittent connection to you.

We often find that friends have other business to tend to. Also, as we mourn we realize that friends cannot empathize with all of our exact feelings and emotions over a loss. Some of your red threads of anger may appear if you expect perfect sympathy. While friends usually do all they possibly can to be supportive, we may feel hurt when their attention shifts away from us. In other words, it is sometimes difficult for us to understand how a friend can turn back to his or her own business so easily. We are often stretched as far as we can go with our own pain, and simply do not always have the ability to extend empathy towards others. A little self-forgiveness for our irritations with those who support us may be beneficial.

If hurt feelings threaten to rupture connections, clear conversations can re-establish the importance of the friendship, and new ground rules for communication can be determined. Try to avoid thinking that you are insatiable because your heart cries out for the caring that you have lost. Needs are not usually insatiable — they can be met.

Sometimes friends or others, who help with your bereavement, feel as if you will benefit by their telling you the story of some awful loss that they lived through. Instead of being an inspiring tale, you may find it burdensome to try to empathically know their suffering and learn from their life lessons. As you listen, you may feel you are not being listened to or heard. When that is so, it is helpful to be clear that you appreciate your connection with them, but feel that a shift to some other topic of conversation would be most helpful for you.

❖ *The most valuable confidant is one who consoles by simply listening and understanding. I encourage you to share this suggestion with your friends so they know how best to help you.*

There are any numbers of social situations you may encounter shortly after a loss. The rituals and memorial events you attend may go smoothly, as most friends and relatives are respectful, and offer genuine support. Sometimes though, we find ourselves in awkward situations, as did Sylvia.

Sylvia: An Outburst

Sylvia was standing in the vestibule of the church, waiting to join her Aunt June. Uncle Floyd had died several days ago, and there were many friends and family standing in small groups as they waited for the service to begin. Suddenly, she heard a distant cousin ask June about a will and talk about what he wanted from his uncle's possessions.

Trying to remain calm, Sylvia turned and said "Aunt June cannot think about it right now but will discuss this with you some other time" and then, before she could contain herself, added "and I think you are incredibly thoughtless for bringing this up at the funeral! I wish you would leave — I never want to see you again!" Sylvia quickly went outside and after a few minutes, realized that blowing up did not help an already uncomfortable conversation. She felt terrible, but could see that the service was starting. A few days later, she called her relative and apologized for her angry outburst. Sylvia now understood better, and told herself that next time, she would be more careful to monitor and contain her emotions and be ready to change the subject or simply excuse herself.

When our reactions to social situations such as this are less than stellar, we can learn to remind ourselves that we are grieving the best we can. There is very little that an honest conversation or a sincere apology doesn't remedy. Part of grieving can involve learning how to communicate directly and realistically as we are able, even if it is just a few words, a short phone call, or a note, to apologize, share a moment of your current experience, and clear the air.

❖ *Remember, in the early days after a loss, your emotions are very near the surface. Looking for short respites through the early mourning rituals is a way for you to grieve as well as possible.*

When we suffer a loss, part of our grief work can be to understand and accept the idea that opportunities for the lost loved one to make amends, solve problems, or become the person we somehow imagined they might evolve into, vanish forever. It is final and real. This may seem obvious, but actually the hardest thing for most of us to accept is the finality of a loss. That realization, of finality, is what makes us reconsider our inner story about our connections, as the lost relationship does continue within the mind.

49

Pedro: A Surprising Thought

Pedro's motorcycle sputtered out. He cranked it again and the cycle started up with a few loud sputters. Pedro was going to his father's funeral and in a nasty mood. That man did not deserve his attention before his illness or after his death. His mother, who he loved, still had scars from abuses before Pedro's father left home altogether. He was going to the cemetery to support her.

A priest who had never known his father read out a general eulogy by the graveside. What the priest said did not seem applicable. Pedro looked on, cynical, holding his mother's hand.

She began to cry and he squeezed. Then to his utter amazement he began to cry. "What!" a voice exclaimed in his mind. He had a fragment of an idea, but it was sudden and clear. No fantasy of return of a "good father" could happen now. He did not miss his real dad, but he did miss what deep down he had hoped could someday, somehow happen. Maybe his mother felt something similar. He squeezed her hand again, and they both cried more. He decided to play her favorite song on his guitar later on. Pedro felt some bitterness leave him as he began to realize that it's the people you know and care about that count.

Another human quality that can be of benefit, even in the midst of almost unbearable pain, is humor. As odd as it may seem, an unexpected situation that in turn, brings a smile can provide a much needed moment of levity. Sometimes, we feel guilty for reacting with a laugh or smile, almost as soon as it happens, but it is all right to find respite in a humorous moment, even at a funeral.

Allen: Comic Relief

Allen's buddies dropped him off at home after a carefree summer day at the Santa Cruz Beach and Boardwalk. The friends were celebrating their recent graduation from high school. It was a long holiday weekend, and Allen and his Dad were looking forward to going to the auto races at nearby Sears Point the next morning.

As the evening wore on, Allen's mother became frantic — her husband had not returned from giving a ride to their neighbor. Late that night, Allen's family received word that he had been killed by a drunk driver. The next afternoon, Allen's buddy called and said "How was your day at the races?" to which Allen replied, "We didn't go because my Dad was killed." The friend said, "Yeah sure, very funny!" and hung up. After a short time, the same two buddies arrived at Allen's front door, pushed through to the living room laughing, and teasingly said "Oh, poor Allen!" Then they looked around the room at all the tearful relatives and realized that the death had really taken place. Allen just stood there, not knowing what to do. Throughout his grieving, Allen thought about his close buddies, the comedy in the midst of the tragedy, and actually felt better, remembering the comic relief his friends had unknowingly provided.

Like Allen, we can appreciate the value of positive emotions in the face of tragedy, and emotions such as these should be encouraged when possible, as they broaden attention away from the narrow focus on dismay.

Rituals of Mourning

Civilization deals with loss and the responsibilities of survivors by using different forms of ritual. Communities and families have embodied certain beliefs about proper rites and what happens or does not happen to bodies or souls after death. From the moment of birth, people learn the need for social connections through known rituals. It may be important for you to engage in conventions that symbolically tell others that an individual or a family is in mourning. Such rituals vary, but some include placing black wreaths on the front door of the family who has suffered a loss, or replacing a blue star signifying each person actively serving in the military with gold stars hung in the front window of a home of a member who has died. These appropriate community rituals serve to show respect for grief.

Another ritual practiced by some is a formal ceremony of the community coming together to support the bereaved financially, physically, and spiritually. Members of the community stay with the bereaved and participate by providing meals and conducting any housework which is needed. They even provide shelter for out of town funeral guests and money to cover the funeral expenses. The key message is "you are not alone."

Clothing also symbolizes grief, most notably the Victorian era's "widow's weeds," the all-black wardrobe traditionally worn by a widow for a full year after the death of her husband. In parts of the East, the color used for death and mourning is white. In some cultures, garments are ripped upon learning of a death. Tearing the fabric is an apt symbol because it represents the fabric of your life that has been torn, and tells others about your condition. Others often wear a special color of cloth indicative of a period of mourning; these are signals that the bereaved person needs a special kind of attention: fewer demands and more help. By asking what cultural or personal ways of acknowledging grief are meaningful to you, you can sort out and clarify those rituals you wish to express or participate in.

Points to Remember

- Recognize "threads." Does the red thread of anger take over too much of a mental "tapestry"? If so, some privacy may usefully contain the threat of irritability, which is in and of itself, "normal." A hostile attitude is the greatest danger to social connections.

- Face the green thread of fear. Use your reasoning ability to look at the differences between realistic appraisals and imaginary suppositions. Try to correct irrational and unhealthy thought sequences.

- Accept the blue thread of sadness and consider its meaning in small doses when it is safe to do so. In each dose try to connect your feelings to concepts about what it may be that you now pine for.

- Use social responses to you as an opportunity to let your family and friends know that you may be feeling vulnerable or even fragile. Tell others you are appreciative of their support and connection, and may want more of it later on, even if right now, you feel you need some time to yourself.

Chapter Four

Telling Others How to Help You
(And How to be Your Own Best Friend)

In this chapter I am going to repeat and elaborate on an important point: you need to revitalize your connections. I am also going to tell you a little more about how to use your conscious thoughts to help your automatic and unconscious processes rebuild your life in the midst of grief.

Others as Helpers

As mentioned earlier, when you are in the midst of reacting to a loss, you can ask others to listen and understand what is transpiring. This, in and of itself, increases a sense of safety and trust that may have disappeared from your world. A caring friend provides an important human connectedness, and keeps us from feeling isolated, or from losing our own inner sense of self-coherence. Being around others, even a pet, promotes some sense of restoration in community identity.

The standard expression in society seems to be "I am sorry for your loss." This is a courteous, tactful thing to say. However, thinking of words or actions that do not offend and have true helping power for you is a difficult challenge for your companions. Those who wish to genuinely help often cast about, feeling awkward because they can't think quickly enough to respond during those inevitable moments.

You can help them adapt to you if you ask your friends to embrace where you are at the present moment. Even if it feels uncomfortable at first, you can make this request without shame or guilt. Most friends want very much to support you in any way they possibly can. In other words, ask friends to listen rather than waiting for them to abruptly give advice or try to convince themselves that they are a great help. That being said, advice from a trusted friend can be helpful if the messages are given at the right time, in the right way, and in the right place.

So here are some things that might be helpful to share with your friends. In doing so, you are helping those who care about you to understand the most meaningful and effective ways to be there for you.

Short-Range Activities Can Be Productive

You may need to be periodically protected from excessive stimulation. Structuring time should emphasize short-term activities and provide a brief break from thinking about the loss. For example, asking a friend to assist you with planning a future organizational activity can, for those who are comfortable with it, provide an immediate way to counteract a sweeping sense of not knowing what to do.

Use Specific Timeframes to Contend with Loss

Intending to use specific periods of time for dose-by-dose coping can restore a sense of personal efficacy when you feel bewildered or overwhelmed. The Scarlet O'Hara approach of "I'll think of that tomorrow" can be adaptive as long as it doesn't become a permanent response. It may help you to explicitly give yourself permission for periods that are respites and periods of facing up to problems or contemplating topics in need of emotional processing. Mention this to a friend who can remind you to limit the time you spend thinking about the loss when they notice that you seem overwhelmed. Ask your friend to "check-in" with you periodically to find out how you are feeling.

Change the Mental and Physical Channel

Activities should include time for respite from emotionally exhausting confrontations with difficult new realities. It is important for you to feel that it is all right to rest, use humor, or change to other activities for a period of restoration. Remind yourself and those around you that positive emotions should be encouraged when possible, as they broaden attention away from the narrow focus on distress.

Share a Physical Activity

Think of something active to do that is flexible in duration, with a beginning and ending location. Or, ask a friend to come up with something. The point is to have a plan, a doable one, and follow it through, gaining a "can do" attitude as well as having the activity itself. Going for a walk is a typical choice.

Expectations at Work: It Takes Awhile to be Fully Productive Again

When it applies, ask a colleague to help you or the associated social group to recognize the all too common expectation in some work environments that you should return to your usual functional level within a relatively short period. The work place provides a continuing interest and social support; you should not be isolated from it, but neither should you have to meet excessive expectations before you are able.

Create a Comfortable and Safe Place

In extreme cases, asking a companion to stay awake and watch over you during sleep can encourage rest.

Because sleep disruption is common, you may associate efforts to sleep with episodes of unpleasant images. It is helpful to increase a sense of safety by doing things like leaving lights on after bedtime. A dog or cat can be comforting and, even if your pet is ordinarily banned from the bed, there could be an exception if you are the one who needs it.

Keep Safety in Mind

You may be more at risk for having an accident while driving or operating machinery. For these reasons, drive only when necessary and avoid hazardous work tasks for a time. If it is important and can't be put off, ask a friend to carry out the task for you.

If you are unsure about completing a task yourself, talk it over with a friend and then make a decision. It is important to do what you can so that you keep your sense of competency as you move through your day-to-day activities.

How to Ask a Friend to Listen

Right after a loss event, your relatives and friends may cluster around and want to know all about it, encouraging repeated recounting of the story of the loss. Later in time, companions may feel tired of hearing about it but you may still feel the need to review what happened. At these later stages, listening is still useful. Here is one of those repeated points I mentioned: just being there and listening fulfills a useful function for you, so tell that to your friends.

If your friends have gone through their own grief, they have experience to share at the right time. Conveying facts can reduce anxieties. You may, for example, presume that intrusive thoughts and feelings are abnormal, and if this happens, you may feel as if you are losing your mind. Friends who have experienced grief can reduce such fears by providing accurate information about how widespread and normal such responses are, as well as the usual course for improvement of such symptoms.

Friends can also remind you that you do not have to dwell on loss all the time. Putting such topics out of mind can restore equilibrium and it does not mean that a lost person will be forgotten.

In the later phases of grief, you can ask friends, if they are willing, to offer more in the way of understanding and empathy. Suggest that they again say to you "I am ready to listen." You can explain to them that by making this offer at the right time, they are opening a door when you are ready. They can also ask such questions as, "What do you miss the most?", and other specific questions such as "How are your new plans for (blank) coming?"

By not encouraging dependency, or rushing in to make suggestions about how to live, they are offering to share in your emotional experience. When they talk about meanings or interpretations, without putting their own beliefs into your mind, they connect with you as helpful confidants through a dark journey.

Though you may feel cloudy, seething, stormy, or numb at times, this readiness for repeated conversations provides you with a dose-by-dose way of dealing with what is missed, and how you are planning for a future life.

Sharing Attitudes

You can remind others that they may have attitudes about what is "proper" or "right" about grieving which do not match yours. Others may have had a different background of etched-in "rules" of good conduct when confronting a loss. Here is where cultural respect is needed, even for attitudes friends or confidants do not understand.

Sometimes your friends can provide useful assistance about something that you are not able to do, such as balancing a checkbook. At other times, they may have to find out important information, because you do not have the energy to do so at that moment. Overall, encourage them to help you stand on your own feet and move forward.

Being Your Own Friend

We all have facets of ourselves in our minds, a repertoire of voices in our consciousness. You want your most reasonable self to be chairman of this inner committee of points of view. In the early stage of grief you can help to start the rebuilding by learning a bit about how you think, and how you can learn to think with your most reasonable self in charge.

It is best to think about the consequences of your loss and how you plan to cope with them in a calm state of mind. To get into a calmer state of mind before contemplating what is now, and what is ahead on your road, you might want to employ a few minutes of relaxation. You probably already know a variety of systems that may be useful for this purpose. If you do not already know how to perform such activities, you can ask others about techniques ranging from breathing exercises to systematic muscular relaxation. These techniques assist the body and mind in slowing down. Thinking about loss tends to make our minds race. Efforts at self-calming can slow down the jumble of thoughts and allow you to better connect them to form your next plan of action.

As mentioned already, in this earlier phase of grief, you may have deflections of your usual mind into more intrusive, numb, or avoidant experiences. The silver lining to your dark clouds is scarce, but these experiences do have something to teach you.

Here is what I mean. You can become more aware of your conscious thinking as a tool you will be using to rebuild a sense of self that may have been feeling a bit crumpled. Let's consider three kinds of consciousness. Let's call the most frequent kind *primary awareness*. We are sensing, thinking, and feeling, and can deploy our attention to past memories, present concepts, and to future expectations. A second kind of consciousness is the *peripheral awareness* of hunches, critiques, and commentaries. You can learn to tune this up by verbalizing what is at the cloudy periphery, which then moves those mental contents into your primary consciousness.

Now we get to *reflective awareness*. This is a kind of mindfulness in which we repeat the streaming ideas and feelings of primary consciousness. Why is this a useful tool? Because in reflective awareness we can put our attitudes into words. As in the conversations discussed earlier in this chapter, in reflective consciousness we can clarify an attitude and that gives us an opportunity to reappraise it. We can consider an alternative attitude. We can re-weigh importance and practice a modified attitude.

During grief, you will discover attitudes you did not quite know you had. You will rebuild by modifying attitudes, including concepts about who you are now, and who you will be. In other words, learn to use conscious thinking, and learn from your abilities to reflect on what is happening in your flow of primary consciousness. Take a friendly and yet commanding stance of yourself, as in "here is where I may make my new choices".

I will discuss this more later. Here is where you start to gain control of your mind, even in the early stages of grief. The results will not be easy, quick, or perfect, but reflection is a tool for best decisions, and you are going to have to become a friend to yourself.

Points to Remember

- The most valuable confidant is one who consoles by simply listening and understanding. Be as specific as possible in communicating your needs and you will do yourself and your trusted confidants a valuable service.

Chapter Five

In the Midst of Grieving: Making Progress in a Middle Phase

The numbness that you may have felt off and on in the earlier stages of grief may have worn off for the most part. You might feel ready to know about and share more of your complex feelings. As you go forward, you will realize some core attitudes that you will be rebuilding, modifying, or perhaps strengthening. These will include concepts about who you are and what you can become.

During this middle phase, it is likely that you will feel waves of acute loneliness and emptiness for the deceased. Many among your support group, family, and friends may have gone back to their normal lives. If you have lost a life partner, you are alone, perhaps for the first time in many years. Yearning is a part of this phase, and it can be painful, especially as these feelings repeat, perhaps intrusively, over days and weeks.

As you face the re-adjustment of being by yourself, returning to work, and dealing with all the social challenges that follow loss, it is likely that you may have periods in which you have difficulty concentrating and have episodes in which you feel more than usually tense or anxious.

Predictable Feelings

Forewarned is forearmed. Expecting distress can enable you to bear it. As discussed earlier, I think it worthwhile, as I add concepts, to repeat some important themes — so let me say again that in addition to sorrow, you may notice that other distressing emotions may come to the surface as well: anger, shame, guilt and fear. Sometimes these emotions propel themselves as intrusive thoughts, memories, fantasies, images, or even bad dreams. These feelings are in and of you, so it helps to acknowledge their presence and to try and label them with words. Words help you keep your reasonable self as chairman of that inner committee of voices that may speak within.

Words raise peripheral consciousness to primary consciousness, and primary consciousness to reflective awareness, which can help you think through distressing episodes of high emotion. In the meanwhile, know that you can get through, day by day, without being overwhelmed or surrendering to hopelessness and helplessness. Also, you may find it useful to clarify attitudes about your plight, including attitudes we might call self-pity.

As the protection of numbness you developed in the earlier phase of grieving diminishes, you may start to feel resentful and sorry for yourself. You may experience pining and sorrow in repeated waves, and if you feel sorry for yourself and your predicament, you may add to the distress. If this is so, it is helpful to remind yourself that everyone sustains losses; it is a part of living, and most especially, an aspect of allowing ourselves to love or cherish others. Part of this reminder is to label states of self pity, because just naming such states as self pity allows you to pull yourself out of this particular pit.

Suppose you have lost a life partner. You may still think of yourself as "we" and the realization that you are no longer part of a couple, but now an "I" can be painful and discouraging. There may be moments in time when you forget your loved one is gone. You may think you hear them working around the house and call for them or think they will answer the doorbell or telephone when it is ringing, and then you may feel anxious, as if you are losing control of your mind. This is a part of the normal feelings we experience during grief work. *Let me also repeat this: the mind is restructuring itself, and that takes time.*

❖ *Because you are in flux, it probably still isn't a good time to make any life-altering decisions, such as a move or buying or selling anything of great value. Try to put off any big decisions for now.*

You may experience some guilt, particularly if the death came at the end of a long illness. You may feel relieved of the burden of being a caregiver and now may feel guilt or shame about those feelings. Remember, the death did not occur because of you, or your thoughts or feelings.

By accepting your insecurities and acknowledging their temporary presence in your life, you also acknowledge that you expect to restore your equilibrium. Remember, the most you can do is to grieve as well as you can, accept your feelings, and avoid harsh self-criticism. Even when you feel sorrowful, struggling to pull yourself up, or taking a few steps forward and then, a step back —

you are making progress. This middle phase takes months or even years.

During this long middle phase, each individual may have unique passages. In general, however, avoidance of some hard memories may alternate with intrusion into your mind of unresolved topics.

Periods of paying attention to other matters to avoid grief related thinking and feeling, could provide a needed respite in this phase of dose-by-dose grieving.

❖ *You don't have to get to the bottom of every troublesome issue, nor do you have to immediately think of a perfect solution to every problem you now face. It is enough to see and understand what you were avoiding and what you will gradually consider.*

With time, you will sort through various unpleasant topics. Grief work is occurring because your unconscious mind works in the background. It may even eventually present your consciously reflective mind with creative solutions to difficult situations. That is why, sometimes, new alternatives seem to "just come to us."

At other times, we can deliberately assess our primary consciousness using our increasing skills at reflective self-awareness. Megan is an example.

Megan

Megan stared into the medicine cabinet. Not finding the allergy medication, she continued looking through all the drawers in the bathroom cabinets she had shared with her husband Gerald for so many years. It had been several months since his death, and once again, Megan was clearly reminded that he wasn't there anymore. Gerald's toiletries were all there, just as they had been on the morning he died. She had not been able to clear his things out of what was now just her bathroom.

As she rummaged around, his favorite cologne came off the vanity, hit the floor, and shattered. Instantly, the familiar scent wafted up and around the room, filling her with a deep longing. Megan began to cry, and exploded, "Damn it! Every time I think I'm making progress, something like this happens and I'm right back where I started!" She managed to clean up the mess, and sat down at the kitchen table. She thought to herself, "I can't go on dreading the job of dealing with Gerald's stuff in the bathroom. At least once a day, I look at his toothbrush, his medications, and his aftershave. I'm tired of this. These reminders have followed me around long enough!" Megan just couldn't face the dreaded task of disposing of Gerald's belongings by herself, but then she remembered an offer her son-in-law, Peter, had made a couple of months earlier to help in any way he could. She called him and said "Hi Pete, its Megan. You know, I can't bear to clear out Dad's personal toiletries, but I think I'm ready to let go of those reminders. I wonder, can you come over this weekend and do it for me?"

The following weekend, Peter and Janie, Megan's daughter, stopped by and used the key Megan left under the flowerpot on the porch to go in and clear out the bathroom. Megan arrived home later that afternoon, and the three of them walked down to Megan's favorite coffee shop for a cup of tea and thick slices of cranberry bread.

As Megan looked around the table, she suddenly realized that she had a living family and that they felt good about helping in a concrete way by dealing with her husband's belongings. She said to herself that she was grieving as well as possible, and that meant reaching out to get a dreaded task done. Megan didn't have to do it all by herself, even though she now felt so alone.

Dose-by-Dose

When I say "dose-by-dose", I mean that when a topic seems too difficult to handle and is leading to an intense, and seemingly out of control emotional mood, set it aside, but do anticipate that you will come back to it. Think, put your attention elsewhere for some time of respite, come back to the topic and think more about it, take some time off, return to the topic, repeat. The key is to pay attention to your degree of emotional control.

Alice

Alice's life partner in middle age was her own mother. While her mother's death was the expected result of a terminal illness, Alice felt surprised by the immensity of her grief. Six weeks had passed.

Alice realized that sometimes she was in a muddled state of mind, feeling numb, and had jumbled thoughts when happening upon a reminder of her mother. Alice's grief work was best done when she was not so muddled and feeling a bit more in control. Alice felt best in the early morning. "Sleep is a great restorer," she thought to herself.

Alice sipped her coffee as she walked her dog, Sadie, around the neighborhood. "It's probably a good thing that I have a reason to struggle around the block," she thought flatly. The bench on her front porch faced a group of large redwoods and she found herself stopping there after her daily walk.

Alice's thoughts wandered as she sat, and it was during those moments that Alice was able to contemplate some difficult topics. She decided to review a memory of yesterday when she saw a memento of her mother and that led to a jumbled state.

Now her first thought was that she might begin to sob. She reached into her mind to gently ask why. Her thoughts then spun into a tangled ball and the sequence ended without conscious decision. Alice sat and waited, and suddenly understood that her medley of feelings, which she now felt in her body, had a simple name: sorrow.

Alice then had another clear thought. Would anyone ever have the constant and unconditional love for her that she had received from her mother? It took Alice a few attempts over several days before she was able to explore the underlying answer. The answer was "probably not". But she had a living memory —she had experienced knowing her fine mother for many years.

The valuable lesson for Alice was the recognition that her body and mind were fully engaged in grief's process, signaling and protectively stopping when needed, and then going forward again. Alice grieved as well as possible by using her mind to consciously push it, explore her emotions, as she was able, and encourage grief's flow.

What do those who grieve stand to learn from trying to manage this balancing act of approach and avoidance? What do they do with insights they gain when they do think about their loss and their reactions to it? How do the choices the bereaved make in the middle phase further the grief process? Each step of contemplating and dealing with the toughest topics is reconstruction of a life narrative, and it is the narration that can rebuild a coherent sense of having a worthwhile identity in an intermittently beautiful and ugly world.

Alice went on in subsequent days. She pined for unconditional maternal love. She did have people who liked, respected and loved her. It was not the same, but it was kind regard and affection, and, it was real, there, and alive. She decided to savor what was available and remember her mother. She planned some new routines to follow each day, small acts that took care of herself, her dog, and her home.

Like Alice, you may have to invent a new routine. It is possible that your creativity and productive self may wane during grief and will emerge once again. A new routine may include a return to your work place for a time, even though you may find it hard to work there in the way you once did.

The place reminds you that you can do it, and soon, you will be able to once again.

❖ *Reality means knowing what is not present, and missing it, as well as recognizing what can be, or is present, in a new view of reality.*

Intrusive Experiences

As some sense of equilibrium returns, unwanted and interfering experiences may creep in to your consciousness, increasing in frequency and intensity. The middle phase of grief contains intrusive experiences which are normal although by their nature, we cannot predict when they will occur. It does help to expect that this will happen.

In an intrusive phase of grieving, each thought, although unbidden and painful, may still, in a small way, be involved in reconstructing your new account, story, and understanding of current reality.

In the fourth century, the Japanese poet and courtier P'An Yueh (Rexroth 1970) wrote "In Mourning for His Dead Wife." The first part of his poem indicated a year had passed since her death, and yet:

"...*Her perfume*

Still haunts the bedroom. Her clothes

Still hang there in the closet.

73

She is always alive in

My dreams. I wake with a start.

She vanishes. And I

Am overwhelmed with sorrow..."

As P'An Yueh wrote his poem and continued on from this initial excerpt, he showed how his mind worked on the difference between then (she is alive) and now (she is not alive). As he moves from dream to reality, he is accepting the finality of his great loss and readjusting to a life that still feels empty of the presence of his life partner. Re-adjusting to life was probably a little easier for Fred, who also had intrusive or involuntary visual images related to his mother.

Fred: Unwanted Images

Fred's mother had been dead for several months. One day, he decided to look through old photographs of her. He looked at the pictures without any particular emotional response. But that night he had a bad dream where he saw himself in a hospital gurney going through painful medical procedures like his mother had endured. After that, even during the day, when he was trying to concentrate on his work at the print shop, images of his mother would come into his mind. In addition, while driving, he would find himself ruminating about whether he had done enough for her before she died.

These intrusive experiences related to the emergence of a guilty theme. Fred displaced his feelings of guilt onto his wife and at times he became irritable and angry at her. He was critical of her because she did not show the unconditional love that his mother had felt for him.

Sometimes, he felt angry at his mother, as if she had deliberately left him. Then he felt ashamed for being so irrationally angry.

Using reflective awareness, Fred realized he was warding off a sense of guilt. He put himself in the role of the person abandoning his mother at a time of need. He sharply criticized himself for being too devoted to his work to visit or call his mother as she would have liked. He fantasized that she was still alive, hovering between life and death, or just "somewhere," unavailable, yet blaming him for neglecting her.

Meanwhile, Fred's wife was very supportive. She discussed the rational and irrational components of this sense of having not done enough. She stayed calm and empathetic, and was able to help him gain an understanding of what was happening. She would also say things like, "Hey Fred, I know you didn't mean to snap at me, it's a tough time and I still love you, so how about a hug." Fred would also say, "Hey, I am not myself today — I am sorry I snapped at you. I think it may be part of the grief I am going through, and I hope to make it up to you. Anyway, you are not to blame, I know that."

Fred sorted out the story of his relationship with his mother. He decided that he could have spent more time with her during her illness, and felt remorseful. He also contained his irrational ideas: he had not abandoned his mother and would not forget her. His wife was not to blame and he vowed to spend all the time he could with her.

Re-examining the Problem of Realizing and Accepting Finality

The unconscious mind is, in a metaphorical sense, the last to know that a loss is real. Unconscious processes may still expect the dead loved one to return, even when one fully recognizes that a loss has taken place. As with P'An Yueh, there may be dreams of return, which are joyous during the dream, but when you wake up, the truth of the loss once again settles in.

The expectation of finding your deceased loved one is strongest in familiar situations of togetherness. These situations, like sitting down for a routine meal, may feel particularly empty. Being alone is so different from the expectations of being together. Cooking a meal for only yourself can painfully emphasize the absence of your regular companion. You will, however, slowly get used to the change and the pain will slowly diminish.

Suzanna Comforts Herself

Suzanna gripped the corroded steel rail along the short canyon from cliff to beach, thinking this was another dreary walk since her life partner, Helena, died months ago. Coming around a bend to a gulf, she saw a stunning cluster of lush, flowering, orange and yellow nasturtiums. Helena loved nasturtiums; it seemed terrible that they could never again share such a beautiful scene.

Suzanna stood and stared, rapt in spite of her loss, her moist eyes said more to her about her grief. Helena had written her a farewell letter and she read and reread the last lines: "love is forever." She thought, nasturtiums bloom again and again. Then Suzanna whispered, nodding, feeling acceptably irrational, "Love is forever." It was good to have a positive memory.

Rebuilding a Sense of Self Coherence

As memories of relationships with the deceased are recomposed, the process may extend to thoughts on the order of "and now what about me, how vulnerable am I?" Hypochondriacal concerns may arise as the loss of the real relationship and its self-stabilizing effects diminish, and if you think of yourself as being vulnerable. A loss can be a narcissistic injury as well as a loss of a "we".

During the middle phase of grief work, losses to yourself are contemplated. No one is immortal, and no one is invulnerable. This realization, intensified by a loss, can lead to both fears and maturation in your understanding of life.

A survivor of a couple may experience the physical symptoms of the disease that killed the partner. This can be a normal anxiety, relieved by the realization that you are healthy. You may feel guilty for worrying about dying when it is your mate who is actually dead. This type of survivor guilt is just one of many common patterns during a normal but severe grief experience.

Unfinished Business

Part of the reconstitution of your identity, and regaining a sense of your solidity, health, and coherence involves the completion of unfinished themes involving the relationship that has been

lost. For example, a common intrusive type of experience in the middle phase of grief is rumination about what was left unsaid to the deceased. Many times, when we have experienced a sudden loss, we feel as if we were cheated out of the chance to converse fully with our departed loved ones.

Sometimes we manage these desires by going to a burial site and speaking to the deceased. It can feel right. Another helpful practice is that of writing letters to a departed loved one. If there is news to impart, or, anything to say, write it in a letter. If something exciting or life changing is planned, include it in a letter. No matter what is done with the letter, whether you keep it to yourself or share it with others, it is a helpful way to express and contain what otherwise can momentarily become an avalanche of emotions or unfinished business.

Although a challenge, gradually directing your attention toward your future is essential for your rebuilding of your own identity. Eventually, you let go of unfinished business and any lingering grievances, not to benefit anyone who has hurt you, but to unburden yourself, to lift your heart.

Reconstruction of Identity

Sometimes, philosophical and spiritual belief systems can help us find a stronger sense of identity. Some of your philosophical and religious beliefs may have been lost as a consequence of a severe loss. For example, Michael felt abandoned and betrayed after praying for the health of his wife, who then promptly died of her breast cancer when they knew of others who had been treated and had gone into remission. Michael then came to the conclusion that his prior spiritual belief was useless because ardent prayer did not work. Michael had much to reconsider and was then able to better understand and then regain the meaning of his spirituality.

Cultural, religious, and philosophical beliefs are often put into a new perspective after a serious loss. At times, you even replace the absence of the other with a new transcendental belief system. You may re-visit a former place of worship or new cultures, and have new kinds of discussions with community spiritual leaders. Learning what others have to say about loss and incorporating some useful views into personal values can help you restore a sense of meaning. Hopefully, in the end, grief will lead you to a new set of principles about life.

As a consequence of grieving, many people realize the preciousness of life and the importance of each present moment, in ways they did not before their grief work. While living life as vigorously as possible, you learn how to replace that which has been lost and aim to develop yourself and rediscover relationships with others. Involvement with others is essential in developing a firmer sense of your own identity.

Remember this: a loss makes us feel isolated for a time, but we are all human and searching for connections to one another. Connections can be re-established and discovered anew as we refuse to give up on life.

Social Challenges: Returning to Work, Interacting with Others

Continuing your social connections and returning to work are not always easy or smooth. Your circle of friends, colleagues and family may want you to be "back to normal" before you are ready. It is likely that there will be awkward moments with colleagues, and stressful periods as you re-adjust to your work and to those you interact with.

Phillip: Adapting to Work Situations

Phillip returned to work in his architectural office about a month after his wife died. For the first few weeks, his colleagues were genuine in asking how he was getting along and listened empathetically. Gradually, though, Phillip noticed that while his co-workers continued to respectfully inquire about how he was doing, they were eager to get past Phillip's inner grieving status and go on to the shared business of the day. When they asked how he was doing, the response they were really looking for was, "I'm doing fine." It wasn't a lack of caring about Phillip, but rather, that the business of living life continues, even as we grieve. A positive response from Phillip ("I'm fine, thank you.") was a green light for them to go ahead, without feeling guilty, resume a normal routine and to be able to count on Phillip to carry on as if he was indeed, doing great! Phillip realized what was happening and put on a normal face at work while he was still, in his mind, in the midst of grieving.

As you progress in your passage through grief, you will find that your understanding of others will increase. In some ways your new status of bereavement may even become threatening to people in your usual community of acquaintances. For example, in some cultures, a woman who has become single again may cause married couples to feel uncomfortable.

Helen: Relationship Offerings in the Midst of Grief

The telephone rang; it was Seth inviting Helen for dinner when he came to town for business. She and her now deceased husband had known Seth during their two years in the military. There had been other invitations on Seth's other trips, all happily accepted.

Seth was now the Chief of Research at a pharmaceutical company and dinners were always at the best restaurants. Seth was witty, charming and gallant, and Helen enjoyed being viewed as "a couple" when she was with him. She was aware that he found her attractive and intelligent. There was an excitement in the air when they were together even though she maintained the friendship and avoided courtship on the few occasions of their meeting when he came to town after her husband's death. When she met Seth for drinks, he said warmly that he found her attractive, but there were no further advances while both avoided courtship gambits. Helen could not help fantasizing what it would be like to go to bed with Seth. She was confused that such thoughts surfaced. These intrusive fantasies disturbed her sense of respectability. How could she be a loyal friend to her dead husband and have these erotic images in her mind?

Helen realized she was now free of her vows to her husband, "until death do us part". Nonetheless, she knew she was in the midst of realizing the finality of her loss, and still rebuilding a sense of who she was "now". Helen decided on a path of restraint, avoiding any sexual involvement with Seth, and signaled to him not to make any sexual overtures to her. She knew she was still in a period of instability in which her long-held values were under some flux. She knew that she was in need of considerable reflection before taking any action.

Helen thought about her own sexual desires and focused her attention on being attractive to others. As she regained a new footing with her sense of identity, she gradually made new plans for dating appropriate men, and maintaining relationships with couples of long acquaintance without the threatening "merry widow" role that otherwise would lead to ostracism or even stigmatization.

Modifying Your Social Circle Expectations

The configuration of any old group of friends has changed forever when you lose your life partner. Pay attention to possible exclusion from your social circle, either because your friends feel awkward extending invitations to you by yourself, or, because you feel like a "third wheel" and decline an invitation from friends when you might have benefited from the connection with them. There is a possibility that friends and acquaintances may make inappropriate comments or, you might be afraid you will make others sad if you accept an invitation from them.

These challenging situations seem to occur after all types of losses. Loss of a business or foreclosure of a home because of non-payment of mortgages can lead to some stigmatization within a circle of not so close friends. Most people around the bereaved person are capable of hearing about the discomfort that the bereaved person may feel. If you are being shunned, speak up and see who will listen. The point is to speak directly about your inner feelings and emotions, and work out how you would like to handle it with the others who are involved.

Sometimes a loss means social isolation. Try to come up with ideas of how to end that situation.

Friday's at Noon with Avery

It was Friday at noon when Matt once again stared at the gray drizzle outside his kitchen window. He felt an empty space in his stomach. Alone as usual since his best friend, Avery, passed on, he opened a can of soup. For years they had met on Fridays at noon to eat lunch at the same cafe. Then they would sit over a chess game for a couple of hours. They really felt fond of one another but Matt had buried Avery eight months ago.

"Pull yourself together," Matt told himself. He put the open but unused can of Campbell's Chicken noodle soup into his refrigerator and placed his still clean, cold pan back on its hook over the center island. He got in his car and drove to the cafe.

There he felt alone, but thoughtful, and then, purposeful. Using his cell phone, he called three acquaintances and got voice messages to leave voice messages. He left the same words to each, "How about lunch to chat when it's convenient for you?" He expected maybe one response. Even so, Matt gave himself an "E" for excellence of effort, as he had learned in his old Navy days with Avery. "My life goes on," he told himself and asked the waiter what was on the menu.

As you move through your grief work and refocus your energy in the present and towards the future, you will become increasingly liberated from the agony of the loss of your loved one.

Even though you are grieving, social expectations and challenges are important to recognize because some connection to people is beneficial in restoring your feeling of well-being and hopeful (or positive) attitude about life. Remember, grief's process takes time, but as you regain yourself, your ability to trust will return once more. In facing what has happened, you can find a way to embrace your future by remembering the good that was shared and thinking about how you might regain some of that in the here and now. Our cherished memories can remain with us as we reflect upon them — planning a future and rebuilding yourself will not disparage the one you have lost.

Points to Remember

- Grief can lead to a kind of biphasic response, which has extremes of avoidance on the one hand and intrusive ruminations on the other hand. This is normal and time limited, but the time can be long.

- Intrusive thoughts may indicate unfinished business and topics that need eventual consideration.

- Work to develop your own reasonable story of "my life story so far."

Chapter Six
Later Phases of Grief

During the later phases of grief, we continue coping with reminders. We may deal with anniversary reactions and other unexpected and even seemingly inexplicable mood swings, normal grief responses that can spring up at any time after the loss of a loved one. Sometimes survivor guilt comes out during later phases in the hard, and normally time consuming workings of the grieving mind.

Anniversary Reactions

An anniversary reaction is a return of strong feelings about a lost loved one on special days. These reactions can be so strong that the grieving person feels the same as when their loved one died. The return of these feelings is not necessarily a setback in the grieving process, and the mood is likely to be quite brief.

Symptoms of an anniversary reaction can include re-experiencing events surrounding the death of a loved one, avoidance — staying away from people and places associated with the event, and nervous and edgy feelings.

Sometimes, a close friend or trusted confidant may notice that something seems "off" and remind you that an anniversary is approaching — a parent's death, the loss of a good friend, or of your having experienced a trauma in the past. An ominous mood could come first. Suddenly, your memory is jogged and it all makes more sense. You then realize that you are having an anniversary reaction which carries forward some more of your grief work in response to a tragic event in your life.

Kelly

Every year, near the end of July, Kelly began feeling anxious, but carried on with her busy life as usual. However, during the first week in August, while noting an engagement on her calendar, she suddenly remembered August 20th, the anniversary of the death of her husband, which took place over two years before. Kelly's thoughts returned to that day and once again, the details of his death flooded her mind. Kelly was disappointed that she wasn't able to stop this intrusive wave of thoughts, and shocked that she could have forgotten such an important event, but she had only blocked the significant date from her consciousness — her unconscious mind knew the time. Kelly instinctively knew that self criticism was not productive and made a mental note to herself. If she heard her critical voice speaking, it was a signal to pay attention, and she would work with her mind to consciously stop it. With practice, she was able to let those negative feelings go.

Anniversaries are powerful occurrences regardless of when you remember them — ahead of time, as a special day approaches, or on the anniversary date. Sometimes, a reaction can take place even a month after the anniversary. This is because on the exact day that a loved one died, you can feel as if you are in danger, and then, as time passes afterward, you feel safe again, and then your emotions come to the surface.

You may feel depressed, anxious or ill but are baffled as to why. It can be difficult to understand why a loss from long ago can have an impact today because you have already mourned the loss over a very long period of time. These reactions are indicators that you need another dose of reasoning about your life so far, what was precious, and what you may want to do to rebuild the future.

Plan ahead. Here are some things you can try in order to prepare yourself, or when you are helping a bereaved person to prepare for anniversary reactions.

Examine your expectations ahead of time.

Attending an event such as a graduation, wedding or funeral can be highly charged. This is a completely normal reaction. In order to prepare, talk to other members of your family to find out what their expectations are. Decide together how you would like to maintain your family traditions while honoring the memory of your loved one. You may wish to add new ways of memorialization.

Confront your feeling of dread about a specific day that may come soon.

Think about positive memories of your relationship with your loved one. Their accomplishments and caring for you can be one of the first things you plan to think about on the special day. You can even practice incorporating an achievement or special quality into your way of living by modeling it and giving the credit to your lost loved one.

Focus on the positives.

Stan's friend made a comment as the anniversary of his wife's death approached: "You showed fantastic endurance going through what you had to endure before and after Sue died. I admire your courage and devotion." The sympathy comforted Stan and he reconsidered the remark several times. It evoked a positive emotion during a difficult period, and it was helpful for Stan to take a few moments to consider the good friends in his life.

Cynthia and Michael

Cynthia and Michael's daughter recently died, and the anniversary of her birth, Thanksgiving Day, was approaching. Family members knew the holiday would be difficult as the day grew near, so they decided to break the pattern, and called the grieving parents to invite them to dinner at a new location. Cynthia and Michael knew the day would be filled with emotion, but they could also look forward to being with family in a new setting.

❖ *Anniversary reactions are painful, but remember this: you would not feel this pain had you not loved the deceased. The reality that you loved another can be a gift you carry within yourself, always.*

Handling Traumatic Reminders

Even in the later phase of grief, it may be wise for you to be prepared for waves of grief and, perhaps, even the sudden flood of emptiness. These emotional reactions may occur when you hear a certain song, smell a familiar scent, drive by a favorite park, walk by a lost loved one's place of work or when celebrating special days. You may become agitated or tense a few weeks or days in advance of a significant day. Realize this is common and allow yourself to experience your emotions and physical reactions.

Mort

Mort was walking alone when he smelled burning wood. He felt a sense of panic, and then he realized why. That had been the smell of his burnt house, the flames out, but with his beloved dog Sally's charred body in the ashes. He felt a wave of sorrow. Then, in his mind, he spoke to himself as a best friend would speak "The horror is past. Sally was a great dog. This was a moment of grief. Walk on. Consider getting another Labrador Retriever." He praised Sally in his mind — what a good dog she had been. Mort's inner voice continued, "And you will be a good master for another pet. People who love dogs are good people."

Signs that you are being affected by traumatic reminders can include a loss of energy, focus, and interest. That feeling of "powerless to make a difference" arises, sometimes invading your self-esteem. One way you can deal with this kind of reaction is by self explanation about what is happening. As with Mort, explanation helps you tolerate distress without being overly afraid of it.

It is important to understand that the most meaningful time is "now" and the relatively short term future. By understanding that you are not singled out in tragedies you can begin to accept the idea that loss, grieving, reacting and carrying on with your life, the best you can, are all part of the human experience. No one can control when loss will take place, or to whom it will happen. Loss is an inevitable part of life. It is beneficial to remember that you are not unique to suffering from bereavement. You are also not a guilty survivor because someone else died.

Survivor Guilt

Survivor guilt happens when a person is convinced that they should have died with other family members or other closely connected people (friends, or buddies in combat), in an accident or disaster, and can result in self defeating patterns of behavior without an awareness of what is bringing about the self impairing conduct. Again, understanding what is happening helps you reduce the unrealistic kind of thinking that is usually at the root of survivor guilt.

Survivor guilt is a common twist in thinking, in which you hold yourself unnecessarily responsible. Less commonly, there may be real elements of blame involved. For example, a person may have been talking on a cell phone while driving a car in an accident that kills a child who was not wearing a seat belt. Then real remorse adds to all the terrible elements of distress. Self-understanding and actions of contrition, reparation, and service to others are needed to reduce the guilt and shame.

Points to Remember

- Plan ahead and be aware of potential emotional triggers. Anniversaries, birthdays and other events that may affect you can be better tolerated by discussing with a trusted confidant how to handle a day that may bring up bouts of emotion.

- Do not minimize responsibility by rationalizing the cause of an event. Think realistically and repeat your reappraisals of what happened. It may be helpful to examine what you can personally do to make the world a better place by volunteering or contributing to worthy causes.

Chapter Seven

Rebuilding Yourself

In this later phase of grief, you may start to feel more comfortable with the security you can provide for yourself and realize that you do have a future to look forward to. By now, your friends and family may be encouraging you to take steps to develop a renewed and interesting life and a future.

The Value of Reflection

One of the principles that can help you move forward is to fully realize that life is not perfect, and then, to focus on realistic choices and already existing blessings given your newly emerging reality. This may seem obvious and simplistic. I repeat it because it's a very important and difficult lesson that many of us struggle to learn.

It's not easy to give up expecting and wanting our old lives back, and for all our desires to be met in the same way as when we shared life in relationship with our lost loved one. There is sorrow in admitting that some dreams you shared together will never come true. We must mourn for that which can never be, but once the reality of the loss is accepted and absorbed, the need to fear the absence of the old dream is gone. The way is opened for new trains of thought and clear decision making. There's room for new hope. Life can once again be happy rather than perfect.

It takes time and thinking, as well as new behaviors, to rebuild all the pieces of yourself. You must set aside time for reflection, new decisions, and time to try out new practices of how to live. You can do this in many ways, such as through scheduled appointments with a professional counselor, in conversations with a trusted friend, or totally on your own. On your own, you may find that the reflective awareness that can occur with putting down your thoughts on paper can help you build a renewed sense of identity.

It is surprising how frequently bereaved persons take up writing, or resume journals they had left behind for many years. Some find that creative writing classes are a way to explore personal issues, as are mutual help groups and contemplative reading about the lives of others. In a sense, we all have recovery work to do, regardless of our habits and behaviors. The loss of a loved one is a life changing experience that can prompt a call for a different clarity, balance and harmony. For all of us, the work is ongoing, and being truthful is important in determining what goals you need to reach as you rebuild yourself.

A Rebuilding Exercise to Try

- Start by Relaxing.

Staying calm and reflective is key. Do not flinch and turn away when an unpleasant facet of yourself arises but acknowledge and appraise it. You are trying to clarify the aspects of yourself and begin the process of revising what does not work given your newly emerging reality. Be willing to stick with the process, although there may be times when you feel shaky about what is happening, unsure if anything is changing.

- Give yourself plenty of time.

Multiple sessions are better than one appraisal. Take a dose-by-dose approach.

- Clarify your ideal qualities, your negative ones, and the more realistic aggregates of beliefs about who you are.

Make a list of your qualities. List making is such a common practice, it's rarely thought of as significant, but a list can be a powerful tool for gaining self-knowledge, a rich source of clarity and growth. A list is private, easy to expand, and can go on and on. It is a summary, an overview, a kind of blueprint that may guide you to the future. Looking down at your list can be like looking down on the whole from a higher place which I have been calling reflective awareness.

❖ *When you use clear repetitions of your beliefs as a tool, you can see the interconnections between various attitudes.*

Look to discover the opposites within you. Questioning yourself can help you see through the layers of your inner world. You might find attitudes about ideal self and also contradictory attitudes about an unwanted self. Perhaps you recognize a part of yourself that is very competitive and ambitious. You're eager to get ahead, but there is also a part of you that likes being liked. You want to be popular at work and tell yourself not to compete. Your ambitious self may conflict with your sociable self, which can give rise to damned –if-you-do/damned-if-you don't dilemmas. You can find a harmony as you sort out your values and decide there is a time and a place, and a right emphasis, for everything within you.

- Reevaluate each attribute or attitude, looking for erroneous, outmoded, or misapplied beliefs.

Aspects of self develop as we mature, but that doesn't mean old aspects get expunged. In your self examination you might find that there is still a part of you that maintains your childhood and adolescent views. Sometimes the characteristics that seemed right and were accepted by your loved one no longer work! There is an opportunity after a loss to reexamine qualities in ourselves that once worked, but are now causing problems.

Ask yourself what messages you received as a kid about how to be: *Be nice. Be strong. Be quiet.* What "don't be" messages were you given? *Don't be a sissy. Don't be a smart aleck. Don't be the center of attention. Don't be like everyone else.* Another means of exploring these depths is to ask yourself what your parents most feared you'd become. *A dropout? A nonchurchgoer? An unemployed freeloader? A corporate robot? A Republican? A Democrat? A childless career woman? A housewife and mother with no career or creative interests?* How did these messages influence your self image? Many of the self-concepts that are developed in early life are worth keeping; some are not. It's good to know the difference.

- **Reassemble the traits that seem realistic.**

The most important tool in your kit for reflective awareness is the kind of repetition and comparison of ideas that can allow you to notice the differences between realistic and unrealistic concepts. This skill of differentiation and judgment rebuilds your executive self — the one that decides, chooses, and governs your self understanding. This exercise provides a kind of central organization from which you can contemplate the interconnections of all your parts. Your opposing views need to be prioritized or compromised, balanced, and aligned with your reassessed goals and values.

- **Make new choices.**

Look for more appropriate attitudes to counteract the beliefs you'd like to change. Arriving at a new understanding and reorganizing your priorities and values can be an encouraging road to greater inner peace. New connections will empower you and increase your self-esteem.

Time Frames

Focus on the future. Part of the work is imagining yourself in various possible futures, with various possible future selves. The past is worth addressing if you are inappropriately projecting it into the present; otherwise you are trying to bottle water that has already gone down the drain.

❖ *Your goal is to use your most realistic self-schema in organizing your thoughts, feelings, and actions, and to keep this realistic self as close to your real self as possible.*

• Practice new actions.

Once you have reworked your extreme beliefs to build a reality-grounded sense of yourself as you are now, you can plan and practice new actions.

Your new attitudes can replace any self-defeating views. It helps to be aware that this may feel like a change, maybe even an awkward change, in your sense of identity. Old patterns, especially those involving your lost loved one, feel normal. Altering them involves actions that will seem unfamiliar until you repeat them often enough so that they feel natural.

Learn By Observing

As we undergo crises, we may also learn the qualities we need to bolster our own individuality through identifying with others. You will automatically take into yourself some of the good attributes of your last life partner. Less automatically, you can observe good qualities in people around you. Copy these qualities rather than envying them in others.

You can think and behave realistically. Keep up your awareness of the actual intentions of those you now interact with. Reality checks, within yourself, or shared with a trusted friend, can provide valuable feedback and keep your point of view balanced and centered.

Personality Traits

Any loss event becomes a part of a life story as it is processed emotionally and cognitively. That being so, it calls attention to pre-existing traits within our personalities. Most of us have some problematic traits before a loss, and dealing with what they mean to us afterward may lead to adaptive work to modify the rough edges of these traits.

Bob

Bob had a history of a deep but troublesome relationship with his mother and he went through difficult adult relationships before he married a woman who provided him with an abiding sense of security in their intimacy. He functioned much better during marriage than before marriage, even at his place of employment. His wife's positive reflections and emotional support made him a better person. Then his wife was killed in a plane crash.

Bob sustained the loss of a vital relationship that had controlled his deep tendency towards a sense of insecurity. The result of the crisis was that he developed social phobias and suffered from panic states and depression, in addition to feeling sorrow about his loss and fear of the future. Bob learned that with time, patience, and work, he could eventually tolerate the loss of someone, retain his positive traits, and help make some of his life decisions in a rational manner. After many months, Bob realized that he was not so dependent, and felt a sense of solidity and self-efficacy on his own. He was ready for a new relationship with a woman.

As a temporary aid, someone like Bob can rely on a partial replacement relationship with a helping figure like a therapist or close friend. Most of us can learn to be alone without panic as well as how to find another person who can provide the kind of emotional support Bob's wife had provided.

Developing a New Life Plan

As discussed earlier in this chapter, grieving usually involves a new assessment and possibly a revision of personal emotional values and your own identity. Current concerns and relationships with living people blend with memories and fantasies involving what was lost. Assembly of your new view of life itself leads to a point of relative completion of your grieving process.

Some grieving for a major loss continues throughout life and may be reactivated by reminders such as anniversaries. Still, relative completion has occurred when your sense of identity without the other person is restored and you begin to feel a readiness for new relationships.

Some of the freedom that is sensed upon completion was well expressed by Mark Wolynn (1986) in his poem "Nothing but Snow." The title word "Nothing" is probably used to mean the absence of unwelcome images and feelings. "Nothing" appears again at the end of the poem. The survivor visits the graveyard where a loved one is buried. Various images are described, then the poem closes with the reference to "nothing," which may mean reaching completion of mourning:

> *Tonight, I go into the graveyard,*
> *Where nothing is loose, not even God,*
> *And under a few stars I shout out,*
> *And wait, and shout again,*
> *My joy insurmountable, as nothing,*
> *Nothing at all, returns.*

The surprise for most is upon seeing the words, "joy insurmountable." You would expect sorrow to feel that nothing returns. But there can be joy that the heavy burden of intrusive feelings and thoughts and the hard review of a relationship are over. Now the relationship lives on in your mind, a cherished memory.

Reconnecting with the World: Getting Involved

By now, you may be ready to reconnect with the world by reuniting with old friends or making new acquaintances, picking up interests that were put on hold, sometimes from before the actual loss took place, or wanting to explore new interests. You may think back to a time when you were part of a group or organization that worked or socialized together, and you had a great time. But circumstances have changed: you were committed to a relationship, everyone moved on with their careers, or if you've been caring for a seriously ill person, you may feel further alienated. You may be concerned that you will end up lonely and while some loneliness is a part of every life, you can actively strive to limit its intensity.

In order to reconnect and establish new relationships, it may help to develop a strategy of sorts. If you're sitting home alone, you're not letting others discover what you have to offer as a friend. In most friendships, the initial connection is sparked by a shared activity or passion. It can help to decide what kind of person you want to be friends with, and then put yourself in a "target-rich environment." For instance, play in a local bowling team, a tennis league, volunteer at a favorite organization, or join a book club. If you realize that you've lost touch with what appeals to you (beyond your family), then go outside your comfort zone and schedule a variety of activities until you find what's right for you and what will put you in a position to meet like-minded people.

This strategy may also create a strong foundation for future intimate relationships. Although it may be too soon to start an intimate association, it is the right time to reach out and cultivate new friendships. Here is one of the points I think it wise to repeat. Anytime can be the right time to reach out to present or former friends. Even though many years have passed and you feel distant from them, reconnecting and rebuilding on your history may provide closeness and renewed comradery. You needn't feel rejected or take it personally if old friends do not respond in a positive way, or at all. It usually means that they are not in a position to reach out or haven't the energy to put towards others. It can be enough to know that you have made the attempt, even when there is no response. There is satisfaction in taking action, even when the outcome isn't what you might expect.

Spirituality

We discussed some beliefs about mortality and what may or may not happen after death, as well as the possible effects of faith, in an earlier chapter focusing on how religion may help with mourning rituals. I'd like to discuss that further, as it is important to many people.

Most people have an intuitive sense of spiritual matters. Personal spiritual paths can range from deep and disciplined involvement with an organized religion to experiences of periodic feelings of meaning and even to an oceanic sense of being beyond a limiting envelope of yourself.

Intellectualism and rationality disrupt such states. Getting caught up in excessively logical philosophizing destroys the simple pleasure of feeling in a state of grace. This state of mind is not based on science. It is purely subjective and fleeting. Faith can bring comfort, reassurance, forgiveness, and support when it is needed. Its value should not be underestimated.

Soulful pursuits are best looked upon as time well spent in a state of grace rather than as a path to an ultimate and permanent state of immortality, omnipotence, or invulnerability to human suffering.

Points to Remember

- As you reorganize your plans for living now and in the future, a sense of competence and self-efficacy will return.

- As you rebuild your goals and re-sort your values, spiritual crises may occur and then be resolved by your own new choices.

- Try to differentiate rational and irrational beliefs about yourself.

- Avoid harsh self-judgments as you clarify your new attitudes about who you are and who you can realistically become.

Chapter Eight

Regaining an Enthusiasm for Life

Recovery of a life worth living after a loss is achievable. You can learn to tolerate the sorrow and move on. Research has shown that people who are able to respond to loss in a flexible way have been able to do so because they have found meaning in the loss, or in spite of it.

Over time, human beings have evolved to have tremendous courage and the ability to cope with each new loss. Each of us, in our own minds, can learn how to become resourceful and build the energy and strength to recover by doing the work of grieving.

❖ *Sorrow helps grief; despair does not. Sorrow says "I mourn"; despair says "I give up." Accepting sorrow means "I can go on; I will never give up."*

Seeing Life through a Fresh Lens

The mind is stubborn, and outdated beliefs tend to hang on. A widow who lost her husband may, for months afterward, say to herself when something interesting happens during everyday life, "I must remember to tell him this tonight." To this automatic idea must be added again and again, "but he is now departed." Gradually, new beliefs develop and the grammar of everyday language changes. A widow will no longer say to friends "we like to go to the beach in the summer" but will say instead, "we <u>used</u> to enjoy going to the beach in the summer" or "I like to go to the beach in the summer" or "I'm looking forward to meeting new friends and going to the beach."

What is important as you set your feet onto the new path of your future is that you get good support and advice from an experienced person whom you regard with trust and affection. When that is not available, you can obtain useful information in a support group whose members have gone through a similar kind of grief. As I have already mentioned, such support groups are provided by hospitals, community mental health centers, and spiritual groups. While it is not for everyone, sharing in a group setting can be therapeutic. Remember though, grieving is an incredibly personal experience. In such groups, you may be further along than members who are in the early stages of their grief. Your experiences will help them, and that will help you to feel effective. Being of help or service to others can also reduce any survivor guilt you may have had.

New Relationships

As grieving proceeds, attitudes change. Of course, you may still feel sad, but it will be a poignant or resigned sadness rather than an alarming level of fear and anger mixed with sorrow. Now you will try out new plans for replacing what was lost. Usually this means forming new connections with other people. You may feel uneasy about reconnecting with friends from before the loss, or have very mixed feelings about beginning a new intimate relationship.

Remember dating as a teenager? You may feel just as scared about knowing how to proceed now.

A little fear is normal and justified. The task of regaining a love life after the loss of an intimate partner is a difficult one. When you have been in a loving relationship, you have expectations which are ingrained. A new person is, by definition, new. The ingrained expectations will have to change to new ones.

You may anticipate that older attitudes may come up in similar but new situations. As mentioned, the prior attitudes may not mesh with real opportunities in the new relationship. Only gradually do most people develop new automatic responses to a new significant other.

Until achieving such poise, you may expect in advance to feel and behave awkwardly from time to time. You might try forging ahead, *as if* you are optimistic and confident, until you learn how to *actually* once again feel optimistic and confident. Boldness is good, but acting in a rash way can be detrimental. By that, I mean pace yourself, examine each person's motives, be aware, but do not retreat into perpetual isolation as a protective stance. Patience and understanding will help to sustain you during a period of trial and error.

Most people need a period of rehearsing and practicing how best to navigate into new waters. I know I am singing that refrain to you over and over. I do so to encourage you to become aware of your own social role expectations. Consider how your new hopes, fears, and expectations fit with the various sub groups in your community circles of acquaintances or potential affiliations. For example, in some cultures, a community might expect an older woman to always view herself as a widow, and to eternally shun the opportunities for intimacy. Yet, she may want to pursue new close relationships.

I also encourage you to take pride in rebuilding your identity. It has been challenged by loss. A grieving process can even help you to gradually integrate previously broken or weak personal characteristics and free you from excessively debilitating habits and dependencies.

You might, for the first time, learn how to cope alone in your day to day life. A wife who was dependent on a husband for financial management can, as a widow, have great success at developing and sticking to a budget or investing funds wisely. A husband who was dependent on his wife can do so as well. Men and women can work on new ways of taking responsibility and actually enjoy a new sense of autonomy. These new aspects of selfhood can provide a silver lining to the very dark clouds that burdened you in the early and middle phases of grief.

It may be that soon, you will find yourself living and feeling well. With the acceptance of your loss, regained confidence in yourself and your direction, and an enthusiasm for the present, you can once again go about the business of living. It's likely that you have reorganized your values and priorities which may provide you with a new sort of map, including newly aligned goals, a realistic view, and hope.

Reaching Out to Others

Community caretaking can serve as a memorial or a personal legacy to a loved one. For example, women who have lost children in car accidents by alcohol and drug intoxicated drivers formed the organization, Mothers Against Drunk Driving (MADD), a highly effective group for changing public policy and increasing connectedness among those with a similar loss. You may want to volunteer for an organization that a departed loved one believed in, or one that is dedicated to finding a cure for a disease.

❖ *Now that you have taken the journey through much of grief's process you might consider helping others specifically with grief. You have gained experience, valuable insight and coping techniques, all especially helpful to pass along.*

You may also reassess your work, whatever it was before your loss, and however well you kept at it afterwards. I hope you had work that sustained you, but for most of us, the energy absorbed in grieving means some abatement in the quality of your work and even time available for work. Use reflective awareness to consider your work plans for the future.

As you consider your future activities, include work that does not pay you money. That is, consider work on home maintenance and possible caretaking responsibilities, as perhaps for grandchildren. What was your productivity before the loss? What happened in the middle phase of your grief? What would you truly like to happen in the near future? You are entitled to think beyond your financial necessities and into the effects of work roles and recognition by work groups on your self esteem, life satisfaction and sense of identity.

Grief scatters the pieces of the jigsaw puzzle that was your pre-grief sense of identity. In the midst of a stormy grief, you may have had experiences of being more aware than usual of your own negative thoughts, harsh judgments ("I am bad"), of depersonalization ("who am I?) or of disassociation ("this new world seems unreal to me! I also am not myself!"). Here is an interesting psychological fact: most of us do not pay attention to our usual positive, consolidated identity. Instead, we do experience its unconscious lapses, which feel consciously like a lack of self-confidence or self-coherence.

As you reassemble the pieces of your jigsaw puzzle you are adding a new harmony. As you rebuild, your positive and realistic sense of yourself will again be relatively unconscious, and those conscious negative experiences will subside.

Points to Remember

- Most people need to make a point of setting up a plan to interact with others, even if it is in very small steps and for very short periods of time. Try to be aware of and acknowledge your progress, step by step, as you gain courage and stamina and embrace your life once again.

- Focus attention on what you can do for yourself and others. Your goal, and the reward, is regaining your sense of competence and solidity.

- New intimate relationships can feel awkward until they become habitual connections. Do not give up on trying. You must be patient and persistent in making the most of realistic opportunities.

- Helping others through similar circumstances provides a meaningful connection. Provide encouragement, avoid criticism, relinquish pity and show understanding.

Chapter Nine

A Personal Story of Grieving

I have a story that may be helpful to you, if you care to read it, and if you think after the opening paragraph it will not be more distressing than helpful. It concerns the death of my former wife Carol from cancer. I told part of this story in another book, *A Course in Happiness*, and I did hear from readers that while sad, the story offered some positive lessons.

It all began one beautiful, sunny, Saturday morning in January. We were enjoying a leisurely breakfast when I looked across the table and saw an odd tinge of yellow in her eyes. From my medical training, I knew this could be a symptom of something serious and I felt the first twinge of concern. I reminded myself it was too soon to jump to negative conclusions but I had a hard time controlling my rising anxiety and my spinning thoughts.

It took a few days and many tests before we knew what we were dealing with — and my worst fears were confirmed. The yellow in Carol's eyes turned out to be jaundice, resulting from a bile duct blocked by a pancreatic cancer that had been silently progressing and was, by this time, advanced. Surgery was recommended, and we consented. Unfortunately, the results weren't what we'd hoped and the prognosis was grim. Carol was given less than six months to live.

That's an estimate, we told each other, only an idea of what our medical team believes may happen. It doesn't have to be true. We decided to try to stay as optimistic as possible while still remaining realistic. We made many decisions about the best way to proceed. Carol started chemotherapy, hoping to hold back the cancer and increase her chances for surviving longer.

In the end, we had a little more than two years together before her death. Two years filled with moments of distress but also meaningful conversations, many celebrations with family, and scores of other precious opportunities to make beautiful memories that I've stored and will cherish for the rest of my life.

In the midst of our sadness, we were happy.

I mean that. While facing the nightmare of terminal illness, knowing loss was inevitable, we still held on to our courage. We had developed a deep sense of fulfillment in our marriage. Our inner harmony wasn't dependent on external events. It came from within, where we had cultivated it through the years by identifying our values, establishing our intimacy, knowing who we were at the deepest levels of our beings, and knowing what was most important to us.

Throughout Carol's final illness, she and I were hurting intensely and terribly frightened, but we weren't paralyzed. Deep within, we were strong enough to cope, stick together, stick it out, and experience different kinds of happiness in the midst of our fear and anticipatory grief.

Facing the facts about Carol's condition was a slow and difficult emotional journey for both of us. Sometimes, in the wee hours of the night, I felt like giving up, although there was nothing I could —or would — do that actually constituted giving up. I knew my feeling was temporary; a phase within a phase, and that it wasn't going to remain a constant state of mind.

Most of the time, we stayed in the present moment without trying to answer the inevitable question "Why is this happening to us?" which is, of course, unanswerable. We spent a lot of quiet time together. We talked about the five adult children we shared in our blended family and our hopes for their futures. We often held hands. We weren't morbid and we didn't ignore death. Carol decided that she wanted to die at home, and she decided when she was ready for hospice care.

Two days before the hospice caretakers moved into our house, she and I went shopping for presents for our grandchildren. Although it hurt Carol to walk, she enjoyed having the mission and deciding on the gifts. We stopped for tea at a little outdoor café. We reminisced. When our romance began, Carol had been a widow for ten years and I was divorced, but we'd been friends for a long time before that. Our friendship had always been the most important foundation of our relationship. We came home that afternoon with a bag of toys and clothing and with hearts full of gratitude and contentment.

Again and again in my work, I've seen that there can be enjoyment in being alive, at least for moments, even under the grimmest circumstances, and that afternoon I experienced it for myself. No story is without beauty and hope, even when it includes the wrenching loss of a beloved. It can be useful after a loss to keep with familiar habits, even those involving chores and daily domestic rituals. The problem with a loss of a life partner is that each home activity may remind one that the partner is no longer there, not away at work, but no longer there as a constant if intermittent companion. In doing each domestic activity I felt a pang of pining for Carol. Still, keeping busy helped— it was a familiar and comforting pattern for me and had been my standard practice of life for decades. Nonetheless I was not returning right away to work. Instead, even though Carol and I had done a lot together as we knew she was dying, I had business to accomplish at home. This was a respite before hitting the empty patch I anticipated in the near future.

In the unfinished business pile there was an envelope with her handwriting telling me to open and read it sometime after she died. I felt ready to do that maybe a couple of weeks later. I knew it was a farewell, not a matter with any time pressure. Her letter ended by telling me she loved me forever. Before that ending, she told me to remodel the kitchen and, as soon as my heart could do it, to remarry. I eventually accomplished both missions that she assigned to me in this letter. She was my wise companion, still present in my mind, though I could no longer expect to find her in that kitchen, where we had so much enjoyed each other's company.

In fact, I was having a hard time with kitchen breakfasts, and I often went out to eat in the company of others — strangers in a café, but still in a "social" enough setting for me to feel connected with others. At the time, we did not have a dog — a rare period in my life without one, and even though I knew I would have a dog in the future, I didn't want one just then. I missed Carol, not a dog, not my children, and not my friends. It was very specific, that yearning, and Carol's presence in my mind was not to be found by reaching outside of my mind, into our, now my, house.

My chores — finances, dealing with her clothes, and writing thank you notes were soon done. I was taking more days off from work, not being fully ready to give the complete emotional attention required of me at the university. Taking care of professional and teaching obligations by phone and email took a little time, but I could also leave home and find free space and new vistas. I did not quite know where to go or what to do, but I had anticipated this moment and had a loose plan. I would pack my car with books, hobby and camping gear, and clothes, and then I would head North, up the coast road. I would stop and do whatever struck me.

My kids had made offers that I might live with them for a time, or even permanently, but I did not want to do that as much as I loved them. The day to "go North" came, and I dragged myself out for breakfast. I decided that when I hit the good cup of coffee I anticipated and felt I needed, and only then, would I decide where my first stop might be. And after that cup of coffee I just hit the road and drove North, not knowing how far up the coast road I would wander.

The Pacific Highway 1 North of San Francisco has magnificent views, provides a sense of space with few people or houses about and is a pleasure to drive. It took me less than an hour before I stopped at an overlook. At the café, I had filled a thermos, so it was time for a second cup of coffee, my limit. I meant for the caffeine to reduce any depressed feelings. I took a short trail I knew from before, to the cliff's edge where I could see about twenty miles up the coast. I had plenty of time, and my eyes were riveted North. I was not too sorrowful to reflect on myself, and about how and why I was reflecting.

Good psychoanalyst that I am, I allowed myself to have "free" associations. I was on a trail that was called "The Owl Trail". In my culture owls are wise and I had felt like a wise owl watching out for Carol's welfare during her final days, and monitoring how our adult children were taking it. Now, hoping I was still the wise owl, I was watching out for myself.

The owl in me asked, "why North?" I seemed to expect something in that direction— not the road or the cafes or the motels or the campgrounds, which were equally good heading South, still along the coast highway.

My conscious plan was to have a time for just me, to grieve but also to reconstitute myself while enjoying an environment I love. On the overlook, I had time to open my mind like a pleated accordion, to allow more inner space for anything that might come to be an understanding, anything emerging within me. I felt safe enough for that.

I thought back to another time in my early twenties when, after a ruptured relationship with a woman I loved, I had gone North, all the way to Alaska. I was alone for a time then, to "find myself". Was I doing that again, I wondered?

As my intuitive thoughts and attitudes continued, one surfaced and became a clear realization. I was expecting, not rationally but as in a kind of dream, to find Carol just over the horizon, not so far as Alaska, but while I was heading North! I was driven to deny her death, to find her again, to just go and somehow do it, as in the Greek play of Orfeo and Euridice—to experience emptiness but after a time, find fullness again, as I had valued for so many years.

Tears came to my eyes. I knew she was in my heart, but not over those gentle hills ahead. I was lonely, and I would be lonely no matter how far North I drove. I felt this sense of grim finality bodily, as if my entire being should be going where I was looking, North. And there was no rational point to that. I would go North and death being final, I would not magically find her there. Then I would come back South, and return to an empty home. But I felt enough courage and stamina to face up to that.

I walked back on the Owl Trail, and got in my car. No feelings were changed. No ideas were erased. My body still wanted to go North. My fantasy reached out to find Carol again, although intellectually, I knew all this and could tell the difference between a catastrophic thought (if I don't go North then Carol will be really dead), a lovely fantasy (if I go North I will realize she is not dead) and reality. I had reality, and I was not frightened of entertaining my illusions.

I drove South, and I noted the experience into a diary entry, which became the source of this draft. I got home, made lunch for one, and recalled another grief related memory.

When my father was on his deathbed, he was 86 years old, clear as a bell, and planned on dying rather than leaving the hospital. When I was a child he had a nickname for me, "Mister Smarty-Pants". Now, I was fifty years old and sitting at his bedside, conversing with him about everything. And then, rather suddenly, and with a gleam in his eye he said, "Well Dr. Smarty-Pants, you are a big world expert on mourning processes. How are you going to feel after I die? I mean, will you have pangs of emotion like you write about?"

I replied yes, but I would not know when they would strike. I was not exempt from what happens during grief.

Points to Remember

You may already know what I am going to say based on your own life experiences. But perhaps you know what you know implicitly. It may help if I say it explicitly here.

- You can and should go on after a loss. It takes courage to carry out the "can" part of that sentence. Should is a word I put in there to mean that going on with life is a kind of built-in moral imperative, part of the human condition.

- Going on means seeking to enjoy being alive even during grim, hard times as well as continuing or re-starting your duty for others.

- The two points I just bulleted above are what a deceased person, such as my former wife Carol, wants for those who survive.

- In the midst of sorrow try to be of good cheer as best you can, or at least hopeful that you can try that in the future. If you believe such a message, pass it forward.

Acknowledgments

I dedicate this work to Carol Ott Horowitz, with whom I began this work. I put it aside during her illness, and for years after her death. I was grieving, not writing about grieving. Now, sustained by my marriage to Renee Binder, I have completed it.

Before all that, work by myself and colleagues was well supported by the University of California, the National Institutes of Mental Health, and John D. and Catherine T. MacArthur Foundation for conducting our research on stress, trauma, bereavement, and the conscious and unconscious mental autonomous processes of healing and psychotherapy change. My most important contributing colleagues were Charles Stinson, Connie Milbrath, Nancy Wilner, Janice Krupnick, Charles Marmar, Daniel Weiss, George Bonnano, Nigel Field, and Are Holen. Thank you!

I am a visual person, and prose requires many versions before it is fit for your consumption. I am especially grateful to Sherri Ortegren for her excellent editing of this work, and both Margarite Salinas and Joanna Gruen for tirelessly going through all those word processing versions, with able editing of their own. Vu Dinh contributed scholarly research. Renee Binder, Chris Benton, and Kitty Moore helped to reshape the final manuscript. *Thanks to all.*

Mardi Horowitz, M.D.
San Francisco
December, 2010

References

Examples of people who do grief work are found in these books, by the author:

Horowitz, M.J. (2005). *Understanding Psychotherapy Change.* Washington. D.C.: American Psychological Association.

Horowitz, M.J. (1997). *Formulation as a Basis for Planning Psychotherapy Treatment.* Washington DC: American Psychiatric Publishing, Inc.

Horowitz, M.J., Marmar, C., Krupnick, J., Kaltreiter, N., Wilner N., and Wallerstein, R., Northvale, N.J.: Aronson (2001). *Personality Styles and Brief Psychotherapy.*

Horowitz, M.J. (2003). *Treatment of Stress Response Syndromes.* Washington D.C.: American Psychiatric Publishing, Inc.

Horowitz, M.J. (2001). *Stress Response Syndromes.* (Fourth edition). Northvale, NJ: Aronson.

Horowitz, M.J. (2009). *A Course in Happiness.* NY: Penguin.

Other Books and Articles of Relevance:

Averill, P. M., & Beck, J. G. (2000) Posttraumatic Stress disorder in older adults: A conceptual review. *Journal of Anxiety Disorders, 14*, 133-156.

Bonanno, G.A. (2009). *The Other Side of Sadness*. New York: Basic Books.

Bonanno, G. A. & Kaltman, S. (1999) Toward an integrative perspective on bereavement, *Psychological Bulletin, 125*, 760-776.

Bonanno, G. A., Wortman, C. B., Lehman, D. R., et al. (2002) Resilience to loss and chronic grief: A prospective study from preloss to 18-month postloss. *Journal of Personality and Social Psychology, 83*, 1150-1164.

Bonanno, G. A., Boerner, K., & Wortman, C. B. (2008) Trajectories of grieving. In Stroebe, M. S., Hansson, R. O., Schut, H. & Stroebe, W., (eds.) *Handbook of bereavement research and practice. Advances in theory and intervention*, 287-308. Washington: American Psychological Association.

Lannen, P.K., et al.: (2008) Unresolved grief in a national sample of bereaved parents: impaired mental and physical health 4 to 9 years later. J Clin Oncol,134, 648-661.

Maccallum, F. and R.A. Bryant (2008) Self-defining memories in complicated grief. *Behav Res Ther*, 46(12): 1311-5.

Maccallum, F. and R.A. Bryant (2009) Impaired autobiographical memory in complicated grief. *Behav Res Ther*.

Maytal, G., et al., (2007) Complicated grief and impaired sleep in patients with bipolar disorder. *Bipolar Disord*, 9(8):913-7.

Melhem, N.M., et al.: (2007) Phenomenology and correlates of complicated grief in children and adolescents. *J Am Acad Child Adolescent Psychiatry*, 46(4):493-9.

Neimeyer, R.: *Grief Therapy: Evidence of Efficacy and Emerging Directions*, 18:352-356.

O'Connor, M. & Elklit, A. (2008) Attachment styles, traumatic events and PTSD: Across-sectional investigation of adult attachment and trauma. *Attachment & Human Development, 10*, 59-71

Parkes, C.M. & Prigerson, H. G. (2009) *Studies of Grief in Adult Life*, Fourth Edition. Routledge: New York

Reynolds, C.F., 3rd, et al.: (1999) Treatment of bereavement-related major depressive episodes in later life: a controlled study of acute and continuation treatment with nortriptyline and interpersonal psychotherapy. *Am J Psychiatry*, 156(2):202-8.

Shear, L., et al.: (2005) Treatment of complicated grief: a randomized controlled trial. *JAMA*, 293(21):2601-8.

Stroebe, M. S., Hansson, R.O., Schut, H. & Stroebe, W. (Eds.). (2008) Handbook of bereavement research and practice. Advances in theory and interventions. Washington, D.C.: American Psychological Association

Stroebe, M.S. & Stroebe, W. (1991) Does "grief work" work? Journal of Consulting & Clinical Psychology, 3, 479-82.

Stroebe, M. S., Stroebe, W., Schut, H., et al. (2002) Does disclosure of emotions facilitate recovery from bereavement? Evidence from Two prospective studies. *Journal of Consulting & Clinical Psychology, 1,* 169-178.

Stroebe, M.S., Schut, Hl, & Stroebe, W. (2005b) Attachment in coping with bereavement: A theoretical integration, *Review of General Psychology, 9,* 48-66.

Stroebe, W., Schut, H. & Stroebe, M. S. (2005a) Grief work, disclosure and counseling: Do they help the bereaved? *Clinical Psychology Review, 4,* 395-414.

Wijngaards-de Meij, L., Stroebe, M., Schut, H., et al. (2008) Parents grieving the loss of their child. Interdependence in

Coping. *British Journal of Clinical Psychology, 47*, 31-42.

Worden, J. W. (2003) *Grief counseling and grief therapy: a handbook for the mental health practitioner. 3rd ed.* Hove, U.K.: Brunner-Routledge.

Zisook, S., Chentsova-Dutton, Y., & Shuchter, S. R. (1998) PTSD following bereavement. *Annals of Clinical Psychiatry, 10,* 157-163.

Web Resources

American Academy of Child and Adolescent Psychiatry

Website: www.aacap.org

Compassionate Friends

A nationwide organization providing support to relatives of children who have died.

Website: www.compassionatefriends.org

Grief Net

 A national organization that deals with grief and loss through an internet community, such as e-mail support groups. *Website*: www.griefnet.org

Healing Heart

A website with resources for grief support that includes monthly newsletter, pen-pals, links, and advice for those whom have lost their children.

Website: www.healingheart.net

Lifemark Group

A web listing for Greif Support Information by region.

Website: www.lifemarkgroup.com/grief_resources.html

Web Listings for Other Mental Health Services

www.supportforfamilies.org/resourceguide/
assessments.html

www.icacademy.org/academics/departments/guidance/
personal_counseling.php

www.stopaids.org/resources/std_info/mental_health.html

Notes

1. Ancient Egyptian Religion. (2009, July 22). In Wikipedia, the free encyclopedia. Retrieved July 23, 2009,from http://en.wikipedia.org/wiki/Ancient_Egyptian_religion# Death.2C_Burial_and the Afterlife

2. Mourning. (2009, July 12). In Wikipedia, the free encyclopedia. Retrieved July 23, 2009, from http://en.wikipedia.org/wiki/Mourning

3. 20 Tips for Good Grieving. From United Mitochondrial Disease Foundation.

4. Stress Management: How to Reduce, Prevent, and Cope with Stress. (2008, December). HelpGuide.org. Retrieved June 19, 2009, from

http://www.helpguide.org/mental/stress_management
_relief_coping.htm

5. "Beware of Pity" (London: Cassell, translated by Phyllis and Trevor Blewitt, 1939):

6. James Agee's "A Death in the Family"

7. John Dryden, in "Threnodia Augustalis (in Moffatt 1982)

8. Emily Dickinson, *Collected Poems of Emily Dickenson.* (1955)

9. The poet and courtier P'An Yueh (Rexroth 1970)

10. Mark Wolynn, *New Yorker* (1986) in his poem "Nothing but Snow."

11. Handel's Messiah

Made in the USA
San Bernardino, CA
02 March 2013